THE CONFIDENT
WOMAN

THE CONFIDENT
WOMAN

START TODAY LIVING BOLDLY AND WITHOUT FEAR

JOYCE MEYER

NEW YORK BOSTON NASHVILLE

FaithWords
Hachette Book Group
1290 Avenue of the Americas
New York, NY 10104

www.faithwords.com

Printed in the United States of America

Originally published in hardcover by Hachette Book Group.

First Trade Edition: February 2010

14

FaithWords is a division of Hachette Book Group, Inc.
The FaithWords name and logo are trademarks of Hachette
Book Group, Inc.

The Library of Congress has cataloged the hardcover edition as follows:

Meyer, Joyce
The confident woman : start today living boldly and without fear /
Joyce Meyer.—1st ed.
p. cm.
Summary: "Joyce Meyer's discussion of the clear steps women must take
in their faith to become confident, assured, and independent in their
walk with God."—Provided by the publisher.
Includes bibliographical references.
ISBN: 978-0-446-53198-6
1. Christian women—Religious life.   2. Self-confidence—Religious
aspects—Christianity.   3. Women—Religious aspects—Christianity.
I. Title.
BV4527.M438 2006
248.8'43—dc22   2006010677

ISBN 978-0-446-55840-2 (pbk.)

CONTENTS

INTRODUCTION

We've Come a Long Way
(But We Still Have a Long Way to Go)

"A woman has to be twice as good as a man to go half as far." —FANNIE HURST

For most of the world's existence, women have not enjoyed being respected properly, nor have they enjoyed their rightful place in society. Although much of that injustice has been corrected in the Western world, there are still many cultures in the world where women are terribly mistreated. This is tragic.

Women are a precious gift from God to the world. They are creative, sensitive, compassionate, intelligent, talented, and according to the Bible, equal to men.

God created man first—but quickly discovered he needed a helper. Not a slave, but a helper. He created a woman from one of Adam's ribs and called her Eve. Note that Eve was taken from Adam's side—from something close to his heart—not the bottom of his feet. Women were never intended to be walked on, disrespected, bullied, or belittled. Eve was created because Adam needed her. God said Adam was not complete without her. It's the same today; men need women, and they need them to be more than a cook, housekeeper, sex partner, or baby-making machine.

Just to be sure that no one misunderstands my comment that Adam was not complete without Eve, let me state clearly that everyone does not have to be married to be complete. And, given that 43% of all first marriages end in divorce—and 60% of remarriages—it's clear that marriage isn't the be-all, end-all of a happy existence.[1]

While most people desire to get married and have a partner for life, God calls and especially enables many men and women to remain single all of their lives. Since this book is written especially to women, I want to say emphatically that as a woman you do not have to be married to enjoy your life and do great things. Just because most women get married, that does not mean something is wrong with you or is missing in your life if you don't.

Men and Women: Working Side By Side

I believe that most women possess a sixth sense that God did not give to men. It's often called women's intuition, and it's no myth. It's the real deal. Here's how it works: Men are usually very logical, while women tend to be more "feeling" oriented. For example, a male manager might look at a job candidate's resume, job application, college GPA, and work history and be ready to hire him, based on the "facts." However, this male manager's female counterpart might be guided more by instinct, by "gut feel." She might evaluate the same candidate and intuitively pick up on personality quirks or subtle-but-destructive attitudes that don't show up on paper. This does not mean that women are innately better leaders than men or that their instincts are based on a special God-to-woman frequency that men aren't tuned into. In fact, a woman's emotions can also get her into trouble, and she frequently needs the left-brain logic of a man to help her see things clearly.

The point is that women and men need each other; they can complement one another—just like the male and female bosses in the example I've just given. Neither the man nor the woman saw the whole picture clearly or completely. That's why men and women should work together, side by side in harmony, respecting one another as equals.

For the sake of order, God instructed that if a woman is married, she should be submissive to her husband. Now, I know that a lot of women don't like that particular "s" word. But think of it this way: You can't have two people driving a car at the same time, wrestling over the steering wheel and competing for the brake pedal. By necessity, one person has to occupy the driver's seat. However, it was never God's intention that women be dominated and made to feel as if their opinions were of no value. (After all, as my husband Dave will tell you, it's great to have someone in the car who can sense when we're lost—and isn't too proud to stop and ask for directions!)

■ How Well Do You Know the World of Women? ■

A few recent nationwide surveys of women yield many intriguing revelations about women. Take the following True/False quiz to see how your experience and attitudes stack up with that of other women.

1. Most American women get adequate sleep every night.
2. Weekends are the only time women get a break from household responsibilities and chores.
3. Most remarriages don't involve children.
4. Most moms say they spend more quality time with their kids than their own mothers spent with them when they were children.
5. The No.1 thing women wish they had more time for is exercise.
6. Most married women are satisfied with the amount of time they spend with their husbands.
7. Time for sex is the No. 1 thing women miss about married life before kids.
8. Most moms say their husbands are the kind of dads they thought they'd be.
9. Most moms say they—not their husbands—are the problem solvers in their families.
10. The vast majority of moms say they don't have enough time for themselves.

Answers to "How Well Do You Know the World of Women?"

1. False. Only 15% of women get at least 8 hours of sleep a night.[2]

2. False. Half of today's women spend their weekends doing chores and attending to other household responsibilities.[3]

3. False. 65% of remarriages involve children from previous marriages.[4]

4. True. 70% of moms say they spend more time with their kids than their own moms did.[5]

5. False. 69% of moms wish they had more time to enjoy fun activities with their kids. Exercise was a close second—at 67%.[6]

6. False. 79% of women want more time with their husbands.[7]

7. False. Today's moms miss time in bed with their husbands, but many more of them miss sleeping in (69%) than sex (22%).[8]

8. True. 56% of moms say their husbands are the dads they envisioned—although they confess that's not always a positive thing. On the other hand, some of the 44% who gave the opposite answer note that their husbands have exceeded their dad-ly expectations.[9]

9. True. This answer might shock some men, but 60% of moms say they are the family problem-solvers.[10]

10. True. An overwhelming 90% of today's moms yearn for more self-time.[11]

Due to years of abuse and a wrong worldview toward women, many of us have lost the confidence God wants us to enjoy. Our society has an epidemic of insecure people in it. This problem causes great difficulty in relationships and is one of the reasons divorce is so prevalent today.

> Ask 21st-century women, "How do you feel about yourself?" and many will confess, "I hate myself."

Ask 21st-century women, "How do you feel about yourself?" and many will confess, "I hate myself." Or, perhaps their opinion of themselves is not that severe, but they will admit they really don't like themselves. Three factors contribute to this negative attitude.

1. A long history of men's mistreatment of women has left many of us with vague feelings that we are somehow "less" than men. Less valuable. Less worthy.
2. Our world has created a false, unrealistic image of what women are supposed to look like and act like. But the truth is that every woman was not created by God to be skinny, with a flawless complexion and long flowing hair. Not every woman was intended to juggle a career as well as all of the other duties of being a wife, mother, citizen, and daughter. Single women should not be made to feel they are missing something because they are not married. Married women should not be made to feel they must have a career to be complete. If they choose to, that is wonderful, but we must have the freedom to be our individual selves.
3. Many women hate themselves and have no self-confidence because they have been abused, rejected, abandoned, or in some way damaged emotionally. Women need to experience a revival of knowing their infinite worth and value. I hope to help initiate just such a revival through this book.

During my childhood, I endured many years of sexual abuse. The abuse profoundly affected my confidence and the image I carried inside of myself. Inwardly I was very fearful, but outwardly I presented myself as a tough, bold person who couldn't care less what others thought of her. I created a "pretend me" so no one would discover the "real me." I was filled with shame and condemnation over something a man had done to me, and I must confess that for many years I held a rather low opinion of men as a result.

Today, however, I believe I am a well-balanced woman. I have a wonderful husband and four grown children. I am the president and founder of a worldwide media ministry that is helping millions of people find salvation through Jesus Christ, as well as freedom and wholeness in their lives. My husband, children, and I all work together in the ministry.

I have learned a lot on my journey about what "true confidence" is, and it will be my great delight to share with you anything I know that can help you be the woman God intends you to be. His desire is that you be bold, courageous, confident, respected, admired, promoted, sought after, and, most of all, loved.

God has a wonderful plan for your life, and I pray that reading this book will help you enter it more fully than ever before. You can hold your head up high and be filled with confidence about yourself and your future. You can be bold and step out to do new things—even things no man or woman has ever done before. You have what it takes!

PART

I

The God-Ordained
Gift of Confidence

Chapter One

CONFIDENCE

What is confidence? I believe confidence is all about being positive concerning what you can do—and not worrying over what you can't do. A confident person is open to learning, because she knows that her confidence allows her to walk through life's doorways, eager to discover what waits on the other side. She knows that every new unknown is a chance to learn more about herself and unleash her abilities.

Confident people do not concentrate on their weaknesses; they develop and maximize their strengths.

For example, on a scale of 1 to 10, I might be a 3 when it comes to playing the piano. Now, if I were to practice long and hard—and if my husband could put up with the racket—I could, maybe, transform myself into a middle-of-the road, level-5 pianist. However, as a public speaker, I might be an 8. So, if I invested my time and effort into this ability, I might just be able to get to a level 10. When you look at it this way, it's easy to see where you need to invest your efforts.

The world is not hungry for mediocrity. We really don't need a bunch of 4s and 5s running around, doing an average job in life. This world needs 10s. I believe everyone can be a 10 at something, but our problem is that we often work so hard on trying to overcome our weakness that we never develop our strengths. Whatever we focus on grows larger in our eyes—too large, in fact. We can turn something into a huge problem when, in reality, it would be a minor nuisance if only we viewed it in perspective with our strengths. For example, let's say you are not a "numbers" kind of person. You struggle to figure out a 15% tip at restaurants, and your checkbook hasn't been balanced since 1987.

You could obsess about your inability to "do the math." You could buy *Math for Dummies* and other books on the subject, and maybe even take a class at the community college. But your math obsession could eat up time that could be devoted to stuff you're great at—like teaching Sunday school, creative writing, or raising funds for charity. In other words, you might rob time and effort from the 10s in your life just to bring a lowly 3 up to a mediocre 5.

Wouldn't it be much better to delegate the math stuff to someone else? Use an online bill-paying system that has built-in ways to catch errors or overdrafts? And you can always ask your dining companions to help you with figuring a tip. There are even tip guides you can carry with you.

I remember interviewing a man and his wife on our ministry's television program. I asked the man, who happened to be a minister, what his weaknesses were. His answer: "You know, I don't concentrate on them. I am sure I have some, but I couldn't tell you right now what they are because I just don't focus on them." I laughingly replied that I would ask his wife later. I was sure she would know his weaknesses, even if he didn't. When she joined us later in the broadcast, I promptly popped that question to her. She replied, "To me, my husband is perfect; I don't focus on his weaknesses. He has so many strengths that I just focus on them and help him be all he can be."

It didn't take me long to understand why these two were so happy and upbeat all the time—and why they had such a wonderful marriage. Confident people make it a habit to think and act positively. Therefore, they enjoy life, and they accomplish a lot.

A person without confidence is like an airplane sitting on a runway with empty fuel tanks. The plane has the ability to fly, but without some fuel, it's not getting off the ground. Confidence is our fuel. Our confidence, our belief that we can succeed, gets us started and helps us finish every challenge we tackle in life. Without confidence, a woman will live in fear and never feel fulfilled.

Confidence allows us to face life with boldness, openness, and honesty. It enables us to live without worry and to feel safe. It enables us to live authentically.

> Confidence allows us to face life with boldness, openness, and honesty. It enables us to live without worry and to feel safe. It enables us to live authentically.

We don't have to pretend to be somebody we're not, because we are secure in who we are—even if we're different from those around us. I firmly believe that confidence gives us permission to be different, to be unique. God has created every person in a unique way, yet most people spend their lives trying to be like someone else—and feeling miserable as a result. Trust me on this: God will never help you be some other person. He wants you to be you! You can be sure of this!

People with low confidence, on the other hand, are not sure about anything. They are double-minded, indecisive people who constantly get frustrated with life. If they do make a decision, they are tormented by self-doubt. They second-guess (and third- and fourth-guess) themselves. As a result, they don't live boldly. They live little, narrow lives, and they miss out on the big, rewarding lives God wants them to enjoy.

You may be aware of some of God's promises for His people—promises for peace, happiness, blessings, and so on. But did you know that all of God's promises are for every person?

That's right—when it comes to fulfilling promises, God does not discriminate. However, He does attach certain conditions to some promises, just as a parent might promise to take a child on an outing as a reward for a good report card.

Similarly, God requires us to approach Him in faith—the deeply held confidence that God is trustworthy and will always make good on His promises. God loves you; He wants you to relax in the knowledge of that love. He wants you to experience the peace of mind that comes from resting in His love and living without the torment of fear and doubt. Too many people cower at the mention of God's name, because they are afraid He is sitting up in heaven, just waiting for them to slip up so that He can punish them. I'm not saying that we never have to face consequences for our actions, but God doesn't delight in punishing us. Instead, He wants to bless us and prosper us. He is merciful and if we are able to receive His mercy, He frequently gives us blessing when actually we legally deserve punishment. Thankfully He sees our heart attitude and our faith in Jesus and not just our actions.

When we have confidence in God and His love and kindness, we can progress to living confidently and enjoying the life He wants for us. Note that I said confidence in God, not in ourselves. Usually, when people think of confidence, they think of self-confidence. Think of how many times you hear TV self-help gurus or athletes urging you to "believe in yourself!" I beg to differ. I want to make it clear, right from the start, that our confidence must be in Christ alone, not in ourselves, not in other people, not in the world or its systems. The Bible states that we are sufficient in Christ's sufficiency (Philippians 4:13), so we might also say that we are confident through Christ's confidence. Or another way to say it would be, "we have self-confidence only because He lives in us and it is His confidence that we draw on."

Imagine you're a member of a basketball team, captained by a point guard who is the most talented and most court-savvy player in the world. Not only can this athlete outplay anyone else on the court, she can also bring out the best in her teammates. You can enter each game with confidence, knowing that your team leader has the knowledge and skill to lead you to victory. Sure, you will need to do your part, fulfill your role on the team, but even if you have an off-game, your superstar will have you covered. She's got your back. And, as each game unfolds, you find that your leader's confidence is contagious. You can play boldly, because your captain inspires you.

So, if I say I am confident, which I frequently do, I don't mean that I am confident in myself or my abilities. I mean that I am confident in my leader, God, and the gifts, talents, and knowledge He has placed in me. I know that without Him I am nothing (John 15:5), but with Him, I can be a champion, because He brings out the best in me.

> . . . *we glory and pride ourselves in Jesus Christ, and put no confidence or dependence [on what we are] in the flesh and on outward privileges and physical advantages and external appearances.* (Philippians 3:3)

Are You Suffering from Confidence Deficiency?

Under-confidence is a condition; it might even be considered a sickness. And just like many other sicknesses, under-confidence is caused by a deficiency of one thing (confidence) and too much of another—in this case—fear. I refer to fear as an emotional virus because it begins as a thought in your head, then affects your emotions and behaviors—just like a flu virus might invade your body via a handshake or a sneeze and then make you feel miserable all over.

Fear is a dangerous virus, because a fearful person has no confidence and can never reach her potential in life. She won't step out of her comfort zone to do anything—especially something new or different. Fear is a cruel ruler, and its subjects live in constant torment.

It breaks my heart when I see people living fearfully, because without confidence, people can never know and experience true joy. The Holy Spirit of God Himself is grieved, because He has been sent into our lives to help us fulfill our God-ordained destinies. But you can't seek out your destiny when you've let fear slam and lock the door of your life. Instead, you cower behind the door, filled with self-hatred, condemnation, fear of rejection, fear of failure, and fear of others.

Many victims of fear end up being people-pleasers, prone to being controlled and manipulated by others. They give up the right to be themselves and usually spend their lives trying to be what they think they ought to be in someone else's eyes.

Sadly, when we try to be something or someone we are not intended to be, we stifle ourselves and God's power in us. When we have confidence, we can reach truly amazing heights; without confidence, even simple accomplishments are beyond our grasp.

Now, you might have read the preceding paragraph—about "amazing heights," and thought to yourself, *Yeah, right, Joyce. I'm not able to do anything amazing. (And I'm scared of heights too.)* Don't despair if you have thoughts like this. Throughout history, God has used ordinary people to do amazing, extraordinary things. Yet, all of them had to take a step of faith first. They had to confidently press forward into the unknown or unfamiliar before making any progress. They had to believe they could do what they were attempting to do. "Achieve" comes before "Believe" in the dictionary, but the order is switched in real life.

It's important to note that, in many cases, successful people have tried many times and failed before they ultimately succeeded. They not only had to begin with confidence, they had to remain confident when every circumstance seemed to shout at them, "Failure! Failure! Failure!"

Consider inventor Thomas Edison. He once said, "I speak without exaggeration when I say that I have constructed three thousand different theories in connection with the electric light, each one of them reasonable and apparently likely to be true. Yet in two cases only did my experiments prove the truth of my theory."

That means that Edison developed 2,998 failed theories en route to arriving at success. In fact, the true story of the light bulb is a long, tedious tale of repeated trial and error. Imagine how Edison must have felt as the failures piled up by the dozens, then the hundreds, then the thousands. Yet, through it all, he kept pressing forward. He believed in his bright idea, so he didn't lose his determination.[1]

Just because ordinary people take steps to accomplish extraordinary things does not mean that they do not feel fear. I believe the Old Testament hero Esther felt fear when she was asked to leave her familiar, comfortable life and enter the king's harem so she could be used by God to save her nation. I believe Joshua felt fear when, after Moses died, he was given the job of taking the Israelites into the Promised Land. I know I had fear when God called me to quit my job and prepare for ministry. I still remember my knees shaking and my legs feeling so weak that I thought I would fall down. I remember the fear I felt then, but it frightens me more now to think of how my life would have turned out had I not faced the fear and pressed forward to do God's will. Fear does not mean you are a coward. It only means that you need to be willing to feel the fear and do what you need to do anyway.

If I would have let the fear I felt stop me, where would I be today? What would I be doing? Would I be happy and fulfilled? Would I be writing a book right now on being a confident woman—or would I be sitting at home, depressed and wondering why my life had been such a disappointment? I believe a lot of unhappy people are individuals who have let fear rule in their lives.

How about you, my dear reader? Are you doing what you really believe you should be doing at this stage in your life, or have you allowed fear and a lack of confidence to prevent you from stepping out into new things—or higher levels of old things? If you don't like your answer, then let me give you some good news: It is never too late to begin again! Don't spend one more day living a narrow life that has room for only you and your fears. Make a decision right now that you will learn to live boldly, aggressively, and confidently. Don't let fear rule you any longer.

It's important to note that you can't just sit around and wait for

> Courage is not the absence of fear; it is action in the presence of fear. Bold people do what they know they should do—not what they feel like doing.

fear to go away. You will have to feel the fear and take action anyway. Or, as John Wayne put it, "Courage is being scared to death, but saddling up anyway." In other words, courage is not the absence of fear; it is action in the presence of fear. Bold people do what they know they should do—not what they feel like doing.

As I write these words, I feel very excited for you. I truly believe this book will be life-changing for many of you who read it. It may be a good reminder for some of you, but for others it will help you step out onto the path of your true life. The life that has been waiting for you since the beginning of time—and the one you may have been missing due to fear and intimidation. Satan is the master of intimidation, but once you realize that he is the one behind all your hesitation, you can take authority over him by simply placing confidence in Jesus Christ and stepping out boldly to be all you can be. God told Joshua, "Fear not, for I am with you." He is sending you that same message today: FEAR NOT! God is with you, and He will never leave you, nor forsake you.

Abraham was told, "God is with you in all that you do" (Genesis 21:22). That sounds like large living to me. Are you ready for a larger life, one that leaves you feeling satisfied and fulfilled? I believe you are, and I want to do everything I can to help you on your journey.

I know what it is like to live in fear. Fear can actually make you sick to your stomach. It can make you so tense and nervous that everyone around you notices that something is wrong; it's that evident in your facial expressions and your body language. What's more, just as confidence is contagious, so is the lack of self-confidence. When we possess no inner confidence, no one else has confidence in us either. Imagine a timid, cowering basketball player, standing in the corner of the court with her arms wrapped around herself. Is anyone going to pass her the ball? Is anybody going to call out plays to her?

When we think people are rejecting us, we feel hurt by them. The basketball player in the example above might think that her teammates hate her or have something against her. But, for fearful, under-confident people, the root of the problem is that they are rejecting themselves. They are rejecting the person God intended them to be.

A Classic Case of Confidence

Just as under-confidence comes with its list of symptoms, the same is true of confidence. A confident person feels safe. She believes she is loved, valuable, cared for, and safe in God's will for her. When we feel safe and secure, it's easy to step out and try new things. During the initial construction on the Golden Gate Bridge, no safety devices were used and twenty-three men fell to their deaths. For the final part of the project, however, a large net was used as a safety precaution. At least ten men fell into it and were saved from certain death. Even more interesting, however, is the fact that 25% more work was accomplished after the net was installed. Why? Because the men had the assurance of their safety, and they were free to wholeheartedly serve the project.[2]

When people feel safe, they are free to take a chance on failing in order to try to succeed. When we know we are loved for ourselves and not just our accomplishments or performance, we no longer need to fear failure. We realize that failing at something does not make us a failure at everything. We are free to explore and find out what we are best suited for. We are free to find our own niche in life, which is not possible without stepping out and finding out. Trial and error is the road to success, and you can't drive that road as long as your car is parked. So get moving, and God will direct you. When people are confident, they try things, and they keep trying until they find a way to be successful in what God has called them to do.

Sure, life can sometimes make us feel like we're in over our heads, but the reality is that, without God, we're always in over our heads.

For example, a little three-year-old girl felt secure in her father's arms as Dad stood in the middle of a swimming pool. But Dad, for fun, began walking slowly toward the deep end, gently chanting, "Deeper and deeper and deeper," as the water rose higher and higher on the child. The girl's face registered increasing degrees of panic, as she held all the more tightly to her father, who, of course, easily touched the bottom. Had the little girl been able to analyze her situation, she'd have realized there was no reason for her increasing fear. The water's depth in ANY part of the pool was over her head. For her, safety anywhere in that pool depended on Dad.

At various points in our lives, all of us feel we're getting "out of our depth" or "in over our heads." There are problems all around: A job is lost, someone dies, there is strife in the family, or a bad report comes from the doctor. When these things happen, our temptation is to panic, because we feel we've lost control. But think about it—just like the child in the pool, the truth is we've never been in control when it comes to life's most crucial elements. We've always been held up by the grace of God, our Father, and that won't change. God is never out of His depth, and therefore we're as safe when we're in life's "deep end" as we were in the kiddie pool.

A Little Godly Confidence Goes a Long Way

Katie Brown weighs only ninety-five pounds, and she is just a bit over five feet tall. She stands a lot taller than that, however, once she's nimbly scaled a 100-foot climbing wall (that's equivalent to a ten-story building).

Katie is a "difficulty climber," an endeavor in which she's a world champion and multiple gold medalist at the "X Games"—which you may have seen televised on networks like ESPN2.

As you might imagine, it's intimidating for a small person to attack climbing walls and cliffs that are twenty times her height, but Katie says that her extreme faith brings her peace, even when facing extremely dangerous challenges.

"I know that I couldn't have done what I've done without being a Christian," she explains. "My faith in God doesn't get rid of my healthy fear or caution when climbing extreme heights, but it does help me deal with it. It takes away a lot of the pressure, because you know that God's not going to condemn you if you don't win. So there's nothing to worry about. When I see others competing, I wonder how I could compete if I didn't have faith in God."

The "walls" you face in your life might not be literal or physical. They might be emotional or relational. And it's okay to feel intimidated or frightened by the walls in your life. As Katie notes, it would be unhealthy not to appreciate the significance of a major challenge.

But, like Katie, you can rest secure in the truth that God will not condemn you if you can't get to the top of your wall—or if it takes you hundreds of attempts. God is more concerned in your faithful effort—an effort built on your confidence in His love for you.[3]

If at First You Don't Succeed, Try, Try Again

I believe that failing is part of every success. As John Maxwell says, "We can fail forward." History is filled with examples of people who are famous for doing great things—yet if we study their lives, we find that they failed miserably before they succeeded. Some of them failed numerous times before they ever succeeded at anything. Their real strength was not their talent as much as it was their tenacity. A person who refuses to give up will always succeed, eventually.

Consider these examples:

- Henry Ford failed and went broke five times before he succeeded.[4]
- NBA superstar Michael Jordan was once cut from his high school basketball team.
- After his first audition, screen legend Fred Astaire received the following assessment from an MGM executive: "Can't act. Slightly bald. Can dance a little."
- Best-selling author Max Lucado had his first book rejected by 14 publishers before finding one that was willing to give him a chance.
- A so-called football expert once said of two-time Super Bowl-winning coach Vince Lombardi, "He possesses minimal football knowledge. Lacks motivation."
- Walt Disney was fired from a newspaper because he lacked ideas. Later, he went bankrupt several times before he built Disneyland.
- Upon his election as U.S. President, Abraham Lincoln was called "a baboon" by a newspaper in Illinois, his home state. The paper went on to say that the American people "would be better off if he were assassinated."
- A young Burt Reynolds was once told he couldn't act. At the same time, his pal Clint Eastwood was told he would never make it in the movies because his Adam's apple was too big.[5]

The people listed in the examples above succeeded in a variety of different endeavors, but they had one thing in common: perseverance. Another shining example of perseverance is renowned pastor John Wesley. Let's take a peek into his diary . . .

Sunday, A.M. May 5

Preached in St. Anne's. Was asked not to come back anymore.

Sunday, P.M. May 5

Preached in St. Jude's. Can't go back there, either.

Sunday, A.M. May 19

Preached in St. Somebody Else's. Deacons called special meeting and said I couldn't return.

Sunday, P.M. May 19

Preached on street. Kicked off street.

Sunday, A.M. May 26

Preached in meadow. Chased out of meadow as bull was turned loose during service.

Sunday, A.M. June 2

Preached out at the edge of town. Kicked off the highway.

Sunday, P.M. June 2

Afternoon, preached in a pasture. Ten thousand people came out to hear me.[6]

You know that Mr. Wesley had to possess perseverance—and a healthy sense of humor—to keep pressing on in the face of rejection and failure. He ultimately succeeded because he had a classic case of confidence. A refusal to give up is one of the symptoms of confidence. I encourage you to keep trying, and if at first you don't succeed, try, try, again!

Chapter Two

SETTING THE RECORD STRAIGHT

God never intended for women to be less than men in anyone's estimation. Neither are they above men. Both genders should work together for the common good of all. The competitive spirit that exists in our society today between men and women is downright foolish. When women began to realize they would have to fight for their rights, some of them became extreme in their attitudes. It seems that we imperfect human beings always live in the ditch on one side or the other. Like a novice driver, we start to run off one side of the road, then over-correct so severely that we end up careening off the other side!

The key to peace between the sexes is balance. Let's see what God has to say about this subject.

A God's-Eye-View of Women

God created women, and He said that everything He created was very good. Learn to believe about yourself what God says about you, not what other people have said about you. God created you, and He looked at you and proclaimed, "Very good!" You are one of God's works of art, and Psalm 139 states all of His works are wonderful. Therefore, you must be wonderful!

Because Eve initially disobeyed God and tempted Adam, women

have gotten a bad rap ever since. I believe Adam should have stepped up to the plate and refused to do what Eve was tempting him to do—instead of doing it and then blaming her for the mess they were in. After all, God did create Adam first, and it was to Adam that He gave the command not to eat of the fruit of the tree of the knowledge of good and evil.

I am sure Adam told Eve about God's command, but it certainly was not her fault that he didn't use discipline when temptation came. Actually, the Bible states that sin came into the world through one man, Adam (Romans 5:12, 1 Corinthians 15:21, 22). I am not making excuses for Eve here. She made a bad choice and needed to take responsibility for her part, but she was not the sole cause of a great sin. It was a team effort.

You know the story: Satan tempted Eve initially and then used her to tempt Adam. Each of them is responsible. Unfortunately, men and women have blamed each other for creating problems since the Garden of Eden. It is time for a change.

Have you ever wondered why Satan approached Eve with his lies, instead of Adam? It may have been because he thought he could play on her emotions easier than Adam's. Although it's not always the case, women are usually more emotionally driven, while men are more logical.

In any case, Satan was successful in getting Eve to do what she knew she was not supposed to do. He lured her into sin through deception, and he's still doing the same thing today to anyone who will listen to him.

When God dealt with what Adam and Eve had done, He dealt not only with them but with Satan also. God said to Satan, "I will put enmity between you and the woman, and between your off-spring and her Offspring; He will bruise and tread your head underfoot and you will lie in wait and bruise His heel" (Genesis 3:15).

Loren Cunningham and David Joel Hamilton make an interesting observation in their book *Why Not Women?*: "Ever since the

Garden of Eden when God told Satan that the Seed of the woman would bruise his head, the devil has been ferociously attacking women all over the world."[1]

Genesis 3 makes it clear that Satan and the woman are at odds with one another. Why? Satan has hated women almost from the beginning, because it was a woman who would ultimately give birth to Jesus Christ, the defeater of Satan and all of his evil works. Just as God said, her offspring bruised his head (his authority).

Looking Back at Women

In ancient Greek mythology and literature, women were often depicted as an evil curse that men must endure. The philosopher Plato, for example, taught that there was no Hades. He said the true punishment of men was to endure women. (Wouldn't you love to see him interviewed on *Oprah*?) He said men could not get into the world without women—but they didn't know how to put up with them after that. Plato is regarded by many as a great philosopher and many of his ideas have influenced our culture. Could it be that some of the lingering attitudes of women can be traced back all the way to 400 B.C.?

In one of the oldest documents of European literature, Homer's *Iliad,* he contends that women were the cause of all strife, suffering, and misery. They were possessions to be won and had no intrinsic value whatsoever.[2]

The poet Hesiod is another guy that wouldn't be invited to speak at a N.O.W. convention. He contended that Zeus, the supreme god in Greek mythology, hated women.[3] Hesiod also claimed that Zeus created women from one of ten sources: a long-haired sow, the evil fox, a dog, the dust of the earth, the sea, the stumbling and obstinate donkey, the weasel, the delicate and long-maned mare, the monkey, or the bee. Not exactly "sugar and spice and everything nice," is it?

To make matters worse, Hesiod painted women as the source of all temptation and evil. To him, women were a curse, created to make men miserable.

> Here's the bottom line: Men need women, and women need men.

From the three examples above, you can see that Western misogyny—the hatred of women—has deep roots. I believe that Satan has methodically taken centuries to build wrong thinking about women into the minds of society. This wrong thinking has caused women to be mistreated, and in turn, has caused women to lack confidence. It seems that women either have no confidence or they are radical feminists trying to correct a real problem in an extremist way that creates more problems than it solves.

Here's the bottom line: Men need women, and women need men. This does not mean that all men and women have to get married, but it does mean that the world needs both men and women in order to run smoothly. God created us to need each other. The radical feminist has the same attitude toward men that men have had toward her in the past. She hates them and feels she can get by without them just fine.

Certainly, women have been abused, maligned, and treated with contempt and disrespect throughout history. But, a bitter, vengeful attitude is not the way to correct this wrong.

Let me take this to a personal level: I was sexually abused by my father for many years. I also suffered abuse at the hands of other men throughout the first 25 years of my life. I developed a hardened attitude toward all men and adapted a harsh, hard manner. I acted like I didn't need anybody. I developed a phony personality that I actually hated, but I played the role because I was terribly afraid of being hurt again—or taken advantage of. Many radical feminists have been abused in ways that are unspeakable. They are hurt, wounded little girls trapped inside adult bodies, afraid to come out for fear of being hurt more.

I understand the feelings of these women. But I want everyone to know that, through God's Word and the help of the Holy Spirit, I was healed in my spirit, emotions, mind, will, and personality. It was a process that unfolded over several years, and I have enough first-hand experience to highly recommend God's ways of restoration and healing, rather than the world's ways. It is much better to let God heal you than to spend your life being bitter about the past.

Shocking Statistics

Around our world, horrible crimes and unspeakable acts happen every day to women and children who are powerless to stop them. One disturbing trend that seems to have increased in strength over the last ten to twenty years is the sex trafficking industry—human beings kidnapped and sold into the sex trade, usually into prostitution rings or worse. The U.S. State Department estimated that in 2004, out of the estimated 600,000 to 800,000 men, women, and children trafficked across international borders each year, approximately 80% are women and girls and up to 50% are minors.[4]

Neary is one of those statistics.[5] She grew up in rural Cambodia. Her parents died when she was a child, and,

in an effort to give her a better life, her sister married her off when she was seventeen. Three months later they went to visit a fishing village. Her husband rented a room in what Neary thought was a guest house. But when she woke the next morning, her husband was gone. The owner of the house told her she had been sold by her husband for $300 and that she was actually in a brothel. For five years, Neary was raped by five to seven men every day. In addition to brutal physical abuse, Neary was infected with HIV and contracted AIDS. The brothel threw her out when she became sick, and she eventually found her way to a local shelter. She died of HIV/AIDS at the age of twenty-three.[5]

It gets worse. It's estimated that between 114 million and 130 million women around the world experience female genital circumcision (FGM), an ancient practice still used today to keep young girls "pure" and controlled by their families. The ritual, which is often life-threatening, makes sexual intercourse or childbearing extremely painful and traumatic experiences. It's mostly practiced in Africa and the Middle East.[6]

Let's bring it closer to home.

Every two and a half minutes, somewhere in America, someone is sexually assaulted and one in six American women has been the victim of an attempted or completed rape. Two-thirds of the rapes that occur are carried out by people that the victim knows.[7]

Ten percent of violent crimes in 2003 including physical assault and battery were committed by the victim's intimate partner and women were typically victimized by intimate partners at a greater rate than men.[8] In the same year, 9% of murder victims were killed by their spouse or intimate partner. The majority of victims, 79% to be exact, were female.[9]

It's important to note that each of the sad, shocking statistics above affects the life of a precious person, created in God's image. We must never see only numbers; we must see people.

We were recently ministering in Africa, and while we were there we visited an outreach program for children affected by the AIDS pandemic. During our visit, we noticed a row of huts on a main street, and one of our hosts pointed out that if a female child could not find food or lodging for the day, she might go to one of these huts to be used as a prostitute in exchange for enough money for food and a bed to sleep in. Many of the girls reduced to this horrible lifestyle were as young as eight and nine years old.

The degradation of women is a worldwide problem. And this problem is at its worst in parts of the world that have no Christian heritage. This tragic situation violates God's standards of fairness. Jesus said there is no more male or female—we are all one in Him

(Galatians 3:28). The total sum of our worth and value is based on who we are in Christ, not whether or not we have a Y chromosome.

Our gender does not determine our value; our God does.

The Women's Rights Movement

We should appreciate the women who have fought for women's rights. The positive changes that have come about since 1848, for example, are wonderful. The women's rights movement began when five women met for tea. Their conversation turned to the situation of women. One of the women, Elizabeth Stanton, poured out her discontent over the limitations placed on women under America's new democracy.[10] After all, she wondered, hadn't the American Revolution been fought seventy years earlier to win freedom from tyranny? The women had taken equal risks as the men, yet they gained no freedom. They still weren't able to take an active role in the new society.

So, these five women decided to convene the world's first Women's Rights Convention. The gathering took place in Seneca Falls, New York, at the Wesleyan Chapel on the nineteenth and twentieth of July in 1848.

In the resulting Declaration of Sentiments, Stanton carefully enumerated areas of life where women were treated unjustly. She used the pattern of the Declaration of Independence and stated, "We hold these truths to be self-evident, that all men *and women* (emphasis added) are created equal; that they are endowed by their Creator with certain inalienable rights; that among these are life, liberty, and the pursuit of happiness."

Stanton's version read, "The history of mankind is a history of repeated injuries and usurpations on the part of man toward woman, having in direct object the establishment of an absolute tyranny over her. To prove this, let facts be submitted to a candid world." Then it went into specifics:

Married women were legally dead in the eyes of the law.

Women were not allowed to vote.

Women had to submit to laws when they had no voice in their formation.

Married women had no property rights.

Husbands had legal power over and responsibility for their wives—to the extent that they could imprison or beat them with impunity.

Divorce and child custody laws favored men, giving no rights to women.

Women had to pay property taxes, but had no representation in the levying of these taxes.

Most occupations were closed to women, and when women did work they were paid only a fraction of what men earned.

Women were not allowed to enter professions such as medicine or law.

Women had no means to gain an education since no college or university would accept women students.

With only a few exceptions, women were not allowed to participate in the affairs of the church.

In other words, women were being robbed of their self-confidence and self-respect, and were made totally dependent on men.

However, change was in the air, and Stanton and her colleagues were hopeful that the future could and would be brighter for women.

Of course, history tells us that the battle for women's rights was long and grueling. Initially, people were shocked and outraged that women were demanding to vote. Even many women were aggressively against it. The newspapers launched a vicious attack on the movement; nevertheless, it continued to grow rapidly.

Where Are We Today?

As we know, women have come a long way, and I personally appreciate those who fought the good fight and paved the way for the freedom I enjoy today. Sad to say, though, discrimination against women is still apparent in many areas. I recently read that in the United States, women still earn only 77% of the salary a man does for doing the same job.[11]

As a woman in ministry I have dealt with my share of criticism and judgment for no reason other than because I am a woman, and according to what many people believe, "Women shouldn't preach or teach God's Word and especially not to men."

I will respond to this contention later and show that God has always used women in ministry. In fact, Psalm 68:11 says, "The Lord gives the word (of power); the women who publish (the news) are a great host."

Because of the lingering discrimination, many women still lack confidence. They live in fear of stepping beyond what they feel is acceptable "female" behavior. I can remember feeling that I wasn't "normal" because I was aggressive, had dreams and goals, and wanted to do great things. I kept trying to settle down and be a "normal" woman, but it just never worked for me. I am glad now that I found courage to do something radical and chase my dreams.

It is time for the truth to be told and for people to realize the attack on women is actually from Satan himself. He works through people, but he is the source of the problem. And his handiwork litters our history. Women have been habitually discriminated against, contrary to God's will. In Genesis, the Bible simply states

"So God created man in His own image, in the image and likeness of God He created him; male and female He created them. And God blessed them and said to them, be fruitful, multiply, and fill the earth and subdue it [using all its vast resources in the service of God and man]; and have dominion over the fish

of the sea, the birds of the air, and over every living creature that moves upon the earth." (Genesis 1:27, 28)

It certainly sounds to me as if God is speaking to the man and woman equally, giving them both rights and authority and telling both of them to live fruitful lives.

We see in other parts of God's Word that He did establish how authority should flow from Him to man and then to woman. The Bible states that the husband is the head of the wife as Christ is the Head of the church. The woman is to submit to her husband as is fitting in the Lord. However, in my estimation and understanding of God's nature, that was never intended to include abuse, control, manipulation, or mistreatment of any kind. In fact, man is instructed in God's Word to love his wife as he loves his own body; to nurture her and treat her kindly and tenderly (Ephesians 5:21–33).

God is a god of order, and He has established lines of authority that allow an orderly, peaceful existence. He expects us to submit to and respect one another. If a married couple can handle themselves the way God intended, their relationship will be wonderful and unbelievably fruitful. However, pride destroys most relationships. It's the great "I" factor. Selfish, self-centered people do whatever they must to get their own way, including abusing those they were intended to nourish and protect.

If a person with authority administers it in a godly way, it becomes a protection and safety net for those under it. But, if an authority figure abuses his or her position, using it for power and personal gain, then those under the authority will resist and rebel, or, at best, they will be filled with resentment. I have a lot of authority, and I have learned that "the boss does not have to be bossy." People admire authority and actually want someone to look up to—as long as they are treated well.

It's clear today that a lot of people don't know how to use their authority with responsibility and love. The statistics regarding child abuse of every kind are staggering—and increasing at an alarming rate. We all ask ourselves, "How could anybody abuse a helpless, innocent child?" Yet, it happens somewhere in the world every minute of every day. Why? Some adults are simply selfish. My father abused me sexually in order to fulfill a selfish sexual desire. He was in authority and no one could stop him; therefore, he did what he wanted to do. He did not consider what the outcome would be for me; he thought only of what he wanted at the moment.

Abuse can take other forms too. Some parents take their frustrations out on their children, verbally and physically, depriving them of the emotional nurturing they need. Children are blamed, accused, resented, and looked at as an inconvenience. Many children are burned, beaten, starved, locked up, and treated in other unbelievably cruel ways. I could tell you story after story that would break your heart, but that is not my purpose for this book. My purpose is to encourage you as women, to tell you that it is time for you to take your rightful place in the family and society. It is time for you to have a healthy self-respect, balanced self-love and a firm, unshakeable confidence in God and the gifts, talents, and abilities that He has placed on the inside of you. You are woman! God loves you, you are equal with men, and you have a destiny. It is high time someone realizes who you really are!

Chapter Three

DOES GOD USE WOMEN IN MINISTRY?

The debate of whether or not it is proper for women to be used in ministry still rages today, at least in some circles. This question is especially touchy: Can a woman pastor a church?

As I address this subject, I want to emphasize from the outset that I am not trying to cast aspersion on men in general, because some men truly support women being used by God. These men have thoroughly studied what the Bible says on the subject and they have learned that God always has, and always will, use women in key leadership roles. I know many men who have actually fought to restore women's rights in the church.

However, there are men—and entire denominations—that are very much against women holding key positions in church leadership, or doing anything that would be defined as preaching or teaching anything more than a children's Sunday school class.

Historically, women have often been allowed to do a lot, if not most, of the praying and servant-type work in the church. Meanwhile, these same men who refused to let them preach or teach stay home and rest.

Visit any typical American church and you'll find more women Sunday school teachers than men. This fact is important, because, if we are to take Paul's famous statement about women needing to be silent in the church literally, then they should not be doing all of this Sunday school teaching. The men should be doing it all.

No wonder most of the women I talk to about this subject are confused about the whole thing. Especially the ones who believe God is calling them to do something for Him, but are being told to do so would be against Scripture. To confuse matters further, most churches today see more women than men attending services and prayer meetings. Pastors often tell me that if the women quit showing up at church and doing so much of the work, most churches could not survive.

> Pastors often tell me that if the women quit showing up at church and doing so much of the work, most churches could not survive.

Again, I want to say I am grateful for the men who actually fight for women's rights and those who have tried to bring a balanced understanding of women's roles in the church. There are many of them, and I appreciate them all. I have been shown respect and honor by thousands of men, but there are still men in positions of spiritual authority who are able to prevent women from taking their proper roles. This makes me sad. Why should women be prevented from fulfilling their God ordained destiny by men who have an oversized ego and refuse to look at everything God has to say about women?

If some men want to have all the authority, they should also take all of the responsibility. Nobody should have authority without also having the responsibility that goes with it. Sad to say, many women are the spiritual head of their home. Some women need their men to rise up and be real men, and I believe that means to be a man who seeks God regularly and leads his family in righteousness and godliness. I certainly know many fine men who are doing that—including my own husband—but I would like to see more men make progress in this area.

I encourage women to pray for their husbands, that they will indeed take their place as the spiritual head of the home. I also encourage women to let men do that without opposing them. Some women say they want their husbands to be the head of the home, but when he tries, they resist him.

How Much Work Are the Critics Doing?

It's a time-tested truth: Most people who criticize others for what they are doing, are usually doing *nothing* themselves. It is sad when people have nothing better to do than criticize those who are trying to do something to make the world a better place.

I recall being a member of one church in which the pastor felt that women should be used only in certain ways. Any woman who wanted to do anything other than pray, clean, or work in the nursery had to present her case to him and the elders for their approval. I was teaching a very successful home Bible study when we began attending the church, and one Sunday as we were leaving the building after the service, the pastor stopped Dave and me. He looked at Dave and said, "Brother, you should be teaching that meeting in your home, not your wife!" Dave and I wanted to be obedient to the authority we were under, so the next few weeks Dave tried to teach and I tried to be quiet. Neither one of us were happy, nor were the people who were attending the study. The pastor had his rules, but the problem was that God had called me to teach, and He had not called Dave in that way. Dave has other wonderful, valuable gifts and is a very important part of our ministry, but he will be the first to tell you that he is not called to teach. Surely if God had not wanted me to teach, He would not have gifted me to do it—and given me a desire to do it. As far as I can discern from Scripture, God is not in the business of frustrating and confusing people.

The pastor I mentioned came from a religious background in which women were not ordained, nor allowed to hold any public office in the church. They were not permitted to teach, preach, or pastor. The thing that is odd is that in most churches where women are not allowed to perform these functions, they are allowed to be missionaries in foreign lands. I cannot figure out how a woman can be a successful missionary and never teach. It is impossible to lead people to Christ without preaching the gospel to them. We may refer to it as "witnessing," but the principal is the same as far as I'm concerned. Of course, I am quite sure that a critic would say it is all right for women to speak about Christ, unless it is in the church, but is the church a building or a living organism consisting of people all over the world who are followers of Jesus Christ? Surely the church is more than brick and mortar with stained glass windows and an organ.

While attending this same church, I also gathered a group of women together and motivated them to go with me once a week to pass out gospel tracts. We put the literature on car windshields and handed them to people in shopping malls and on street corners. In a few weeks, we had distributed ten thousand gospel tracts, for no other reason than we wanted to serve God. I was called before the elders and corrected publicly for distributing this material without the elders' permission.

Those who criticized me did not want to help me get the tracts out, but they did want to stop me. I am sorry to have to say this, but I believe their disapproval was nothing more than male ego. They saw a woman doing what they should have been doing, so they found fault with me in order to soothe their own guilty consciences.

Women in Ministry: A God-Ordained Tradition

Whether we look at Miriam, Deborah, Esther, and Ruth in the Old Testament—or Mary the mother of Jesus, Mary Magdalene, or Priscilla in the New Testament, we easily see that God has always used women in ministry. When He needed someone to save the Jews from the destruction that wicked Haman had planned for them, He called upon Esther (Esther 4:14b). If God is against using women, why didn't He call a man for this job? Esther sacrificed her plans as a young woman and allowed herself to be taken into the king's harem in order to be in a position to speak on behalf of God's people when the time came to do so. Because of her obedience, God gave her favor with the king, and she exposed a plot to kill all of the Jews. She saved her nation and

> If God did not want to use women in ministry, why did He include them in the most important events in Jesus' life?

became a queen who held a high position of leadership in the land and cared for the poor.

Deborah was a prophetess and a judge. As a prophetess, she was a spokesperson for God. As a judge she made decisions on God's behalf (Judges 4:5).

Mary Magdalene and some other women were the first to visit the tomb on Resurrection Sunday (John 20:1). They found the tomb empty, but an angel appeared to them and gave these instructions, "Go and tell His disciples that He is arisen." "Go and tell." Sounds to me like the preaching of the Gospel. Actually, Luke records that when Mary and her friends found the other disciples, it was the disciples who didn't believe that Jesus had risen from the dead and the tomb was empty. I wonder why some of them had not already been to the tomb? Why was it just the women who ventured out?

A woman gave birth to our Savior, and many women helped care for and support Jesus during His life and ministry. Women were at the cross when He died, and first at the empty tomb. If God did not want to use women in ministry, why did He include them in the most important events in Jesus' life?

It seems to me that God gave women a place of honor—rather than excluding them like some men have tried to do.

Want more examples? Priscilla and her husband, Aquila, had a church in their home and since she is mentioned equally with him, she must have pastored the church alongside him (Acts 18:2–26). Interestingly, her name is listed first, which some scholars say may indicate that she had a larger pastoral role than her husband.

Women ministered both to and with Jesus. The same Greek verb that is translated deacon and applied to seven men in the New Testament is also applied to seven women. They are: Peter's mother-in-law; Mary Magdalene; Mary, the mother of James and Joses; Salome, the mother of Zebedee's children; Joanna, the wife of Chuza; Susanna; and Martha, the sister of Mary and Lazarus.

When Luke mentions the travels of Jesus, he also mentions the twelve men who were with Him, and some women. Is it possible that these women had a publicly recognized role similar to that of the men? At least one scholar believes they did. These women provided for Jesus from their belongings, according to Luke (Luke 8:3).

When the 120 people gathered in the upper room on the day of Pentecost, the count included women (Acts 1:14, 15). If women did not need power to spread the gospel, why were they included in the outpouring of the Holy Spirit? Acts 1:8 states clearly that "when the Holy Spirit has come upon you, you shall receive power to be my witnesses in Jerusalem, Judea and to the ends of the earth."

When Joel prophesied about the future outpouring of the Holy Spirit, he said that God would pour His spirit out upon all flesh. Upon his menservants and his maidservants He would pour His spirit out (Joel 2:28, 29). He said that "they" would prophesy. He did not just say that men would prophesy. To prophesy can mean the same thing as teaching and preaching. It simply means to speak forth the inspired word of God.

Of the thirty-nine co-workers that Paul mentioned throughout his writings, at least one-fourth were women. In Philippians 4, Paul encourages Euodia and Syntyche to keep cooperating and states that they had toiled along with him in spreading the good news of the gospel.

Beyond the preceding examples from the Bible, I could create a very long list of women who have been successfully used throughout church history to do major things in God's kingdom. Just a few are Julian of Norwich, Madam Guyon, Joan of Arc, Aimee Semple McPherson, Kathryn Kuhlman, Maria Woodworth Etter, Mother Teresa, Catherine Booth of the Salvation Army, Corrie ten Boom, and Joni Eareckson Tada.

But, What About Paul?

Let a woman learn in quietness, in entire submissiveness.
I allow no woman to teach or to have authority over
men; she is to remain in quietness and keep silence
[in religious assemblies]. (1 Timothy 2:11, 12)

In almost every interview I do, I am asked what I think about what Paul said about women keeping quiet in the church and not being allowed to teach men. Thankfully, after I am finished with this book, I can simply tell people to get a copy prior to the interview. Then they'll know what I think.

First, we must realize that there are absolute truths in Scripture, and then there are truths that are relative to the times they were written in. In 1 Corinthians 14, when Paul told the women to be silent, he had already told two other groups to be silent. They were those who spoke in tongues and those who prophesied (see 1 Corinthians 14:28, 32, 34). All of these instructions were intended to bring order to the service—not to silence the people forever or prevent them from teaching and preaching the gospel of Jesus Christ. To be honest, given that so many people need to hear the gospel, I cannot imagine God forbidding any willing person to preach it. The Lord has instructed us to pray that He would send laborers out into the harvest. He said the harvest is ripe and the laborers are few (Luke 10:2). He did not say, "Pray that I will send male laborers into the harvest."

Now, back to our troublesome passage from Paul. It appears that those who spoke in tongues, those who prophesied, and some of the women were all disrupting the service for various reasons. They lacked self-control, and they were not using wisdom to know when to speak out. The women were uneducated and may have been asking questions at inappropriate times. Many of the people becoming Christians had been involved in pagan worship, which included an abundance of loud noises during their worship of pagan gods. It is possible, according to some scholars, that some of the women may have reverted to some of their pagan ways in their excitement and enthusiasm.

With this background, let's take a better look at what Paul said.

> *The women should keep quiet in the churches, for they are not authorized to speak, but should take a secondary and subordinate place, just as the Law also says.*
>
> *But if there is anything they want to learn, they should ask their own husbands at home, for it is disgraceful for a woman to talk in church [for her to usurp and exercise authority over men in the church].*
>
> *What! Did the word of the Lord originate with you [Corinthians], or has it reached only you?* (1 Corinthians 14:34–36)

The Corinthian church and Paul wrote letters back and forth with the church leaders asking questions, and Paul answering them. Some scholars point out that Paul seems to repeat a question asked by the Corinthians in verses 34 and 35—and then in verse 36 responds with, "What! Did the word of the Lord originate with you (Corinthians) or has it reached only you?" Notice the exclamation point after the word "what." It seems Paul sounds surprised at their question and reminds them that God's Word has come for all people. I tend to agree with this line of thinking; otherwise Paul's comment in verse 36 makes no sense. He goes on to explain that the Corinthians should earnestly desire and set their hearts on prophesying, speaking in tongues, and interpreting— and not forbid or hinder those gifts. He concludes by saying that all things should be done with regard to decency and propriety and in an orderly fashion.

You may have noticed that Paul did say that women should not usurp authority over men. It is true that some women who teach or preach may develop a wrong attitude. They may think their position allows them to exercise authority over people. I cannot be responsible for what other women do, but as for me, I can honestly say that when I teach God's Word, I don't see myself exercising authority over men or women. I simply use the gift of communication that God has given me to fulfill the call on my life to teach. I want to help people understand God's Word so they can easily apply it to their daily lives. When I hold a public meeting, I believe I have authority over that meeting and that I am responsible to keep order, but, once again, I have never felt that I was taking authority over people. The Corinthian church may have been dealing with a woman or some women who had an unscriptural attitude, but all women should not be permanently punished for it.

It is difficult to know exactly what was going on when Paul wrote this letter, but we cannot take this verse to mean that women were forever forbidden to speak in church. We must look at all of the other Scriptures which clearly indicate that God regularly used women.

Also, Paul recognized women and their right to learn and be educated when he told them to learn from their husbands at home. As I've said before, I believe his comment to keep silent in the church was intended to keep order, not prevent women from participating properly. They were simply to subordinate themselves to the authority present, just as others were expected to do.

In 1 Corinthians 11:5, Paul gave instructions for a woman to have her head covered when she prayed or prophesied publicly (teaches, refutes, reproves, admonishes or comforts). Why would Paul instruct a woman in how to dress when she prayed or prophesied (remember, part of the definition of prophesying means to teach), if he required women to always keep silent in the church? It is impossible to prophesy and keep silent at the same time. (Incidentally, it was the custom of the day for women to cover their heads during these times as a sign of respect and submission to authority. That is no longer a custom in our society, and is not something women are taught they have to do.)

So, to recap: In 1 Timothy 2, Paul said that he allowed no women to teach. This one verse has prevented many thousands of women from answering their God-ordained destiny over the years. Priscilla along with her husband, Aquila, was a founding leader in this same church that Paul was writing to. Given that fact, did he really intend that women should keep silent and not teach? Was Paul saying women could never be leaders in the church, when he was the one who asked the church in Rome to receive the woman minister Phoebe with all due respect and honor (Romans 16:1, 2)?

We may never know exactly what Paul was dealing with and why he expressed himself the way he did in this controversial passage, but it is evident that he was dealing with a specific situation for a specific timeframe in history—one that was not intended to be a "forever" rule.

Remember, Paul said in 1 Timothy 2:9 that women should adorn themselves modestly and appropriately and sensibly; not with elaborate hair arrangements or gold or pearls or expensive clothing. Does that mean that any woman today who wears gold or pearls is disobeying what Paul said? This is not the case at all, because once again we see that what Paul wrote was due to specific situations regarding the customs of the day. The Romans prized pearls above all other jewelry, and wearing them was a most-ostentatious display of vanity. Paul felt that the Christian women should not do anything that would cause them to look worldly. Ephesus was a sinful city, and women who wore fancy jewelry and clothing or who had fancy hair arrangements were considered to be

> Don't let anyone ever tell you that God cannot or will not use you, just because you are a woman.

vain, if not downright immoral. Paul wanted women to concentrate on inner beauty more than outward appearance.

If we are trapped in all of the customs of the days when Paul wrote his letters, then men should wear robes or tunics, because in those days they did not wear pants. Styles change, times change, and let me say once again that a lot of what Paul said regarding women is relative to a specific time in church history. And that time has passed.

Finally, let me say that some scholars believe Paul was speaking to a specific woman who was deceived and out of order. He wanted her to learn the proper way to handle herself, but it had to be at home and not during the church service. Until she did learn, she was forbidden to speak in the church or to teach in any way.

I am not enough of a theologian to debate this problem fully. I have read a great deal of what others more educated than myself have written, and I have endeavored to share, in part, what I feel I have learned from them. All I know is that God has always used—and still does use—women as leaders and teachers, preachers, ministers, missionaries, authors, evangelists, prophets, and so on. You will find a list at the end of this chapter of other books on this subject you might consider reading if you feel you want more information than I have included in this section.

Just remember that God loves you and wants to use you in powerful ways to help other people. Don't ever let anyone tell you that God cannot or will not use you, just because you are a woman. As a woman, you are creative, comforting, sensitive, and you're able to be a tremendous blessing. You can bear a lot of good fruit in your life. You don't have to merely pass through life unnoticed, always in the background. If God has called you to leadership, then you should lead. If He has called you into ministry, then you should minister. If He has called you to business or as a home-maker, then you should boldly be all that He has called you to be.

Recommended Resources

Why Not Women? A Fresh Look at Scripture on Women in Missions, Ministry and Leadership, by Loren Cunningham and David Joel Hamilton with Janice Rogers. YWAM Publishing, 2000.

Are Women Human?, by Dorothy L. Sayers, William B. Eermans Publishing Company, Grand Rapids, 1971.

Beyond Sex Roles: What the Bible Says About a Woman's Place in Church and Family, by Gilbert Bilezikian, Baker Book House, Grand Rapids, Second Edition, 1993.

Female Ministry: Woman's Right to Preach the Gospel, by Catherine Booth, The Salvation Army Supplies Printing and Publishing Department, New York, 1859, reprinted 1975.

What Paul Really Said About Women: An Apostle's Liberating View on Equality in Marriage, Leadership, and Love, by John Temple Bristow, Harper and Row, San Francisco, 1988.

Who Said Women Can't Teach?, by Charles Trombley, Bridge Publishing, Inc., South Plainfield, 1985.

Chapter Four

SEVEN SECRETS OF A CONFIDENT WOMAN

Every cause has an effect. If some women are confident while others are not, there must be reasons. I want to examine some of them to help you tap into things that may help you live more confidently and boldly.

SECRET # 1—A confident woman knows that she is loved.

She does not fear being unloved, because she knows first and foremost that God loves her unconditionally. To be whole and complete, we need to know that we are loved. Everyone desires and needs love and acceptance from God and others. Although not everyone will accept and love us, some will. I encourage you to concentrate on those who do love you and forget about those who don't. God certainly does love us, and He can provide others who do as well—if we'll look to Him and stop making bad choices about whom we bring into our circle of inclusion. I believe we need to have what I call "divine connections." In other words, pray about your circle of friends. Don't just decide what social group you want to be part of and then try to get into it. Instead, follow the leading of the Holy Spirit in choosing with whom you want to associate closely.

There are women who feel so bad about themselves that they get involved with men who will hurt them, because they believe that is all they deserve. You need to be around safe people, not

Love is the healing balm that the world needs, and God offers it freely and continuously.

people who continue to wound you. God will help you learn to recognize those people if you listen to His wisdom.

The first place to start if you need to be loved is with God. He is a Father who wants to shower love and blessings upon His children. If your natural father did not love you properly, you can now get from God what you missed in your childhood. Love is the healing balm that the world needs, and God offers it freely and continuously. His love is unconditional. He does not love us IF; He simply and for all time loves us. He does not love us because we deserve it; He loves us because He is kind and wants to.

> *Even as [in His love] He chose us [actually picked us out for Himself as His own] in Christ before the foundation of the world, that we should be holy [consecrated and set apart for Him] and blameless in His sight, even above reproach, before Him in love.*
>
> *For He foreordained us [destined us, planned in love for us] to be adopted [revealed] as His own children through Jesus Christ, in accordance with the purpose of His will [because it pleased Him and was His kind intent].* (Ephesians 1:4, 5)

In all of my books, I include something about the love of God and how important it is for us to receive it fully. I do this because I believe receiving the free gift of God's unconditional love is the beginning of our healing, and the foundation for our new life in Christ. We cannot love ourselves unless we realize how much God loves us, and if we don't love ourselves, we cannot love other people. We cannot maintain good, healthy relationships without this foundation of love in our lives.

Many people fail at marriage because they simply don't love

themselves, and therefore they have nothing to give in the relationship. They spend most of their time trying to get from their spouses what only God can give them, which is a sense of their own worth and value.

I grew up in an abusive, dysfunctional atmosphere and was filled with shame, blame, and disgrace by the time I was eighteen. I married very young simply because I was afraid no one would ever want me. A boy of nineteen showed an interest in me, and although I didn't even know what love was, I married him because I was desperate. He had problems of his own and did not really know how to love me—so the pattern of pain in my life continued. I was repeatedly hurt in that relationship, which ended in divorce after five years.

By the time I met the man I have now been married to since 1967, I was desperate for love but did not know how to receive it, even when it was available. Dave (my husband) really did love me, but I found myself constantly deflecting his love due to the way I felt about myself down deep inside. As I entered into a serious and committed relationship with God, through Jesus Christ, I began to learn about God's love. But it took a long time to fully accept it. When you feel unlovable, it is hard to get it through your head and down into your heart that God loves you perfectly—even though you are not perfect and never will be as long as you are on the earth.

There is only one thing you can do with a free gift, and that is receive it and be grateful. I urge you to take a step of faith right now and say out loud, "God loves me unconditionally, and I receive His love!" You may have to say it a hundred times a day, like I did for months, before it finally sinks in, but when it does it will be the happiest day of your life. To know that you are loved by someone you can trust is the best and most comforting feeling in the world. God will not only love you that way, but He will also provide other people who will truly love you. When He does provide, be sure to remain thankful for those people. Having people who genuinely love you is one of the most precious gifts in the world.

The Bible says in 1 John 4:18 that the perfect love of God casts out fear. When fear does not rule us, we are free to be bold and confident.

God loves you! God loves you! God loves you! Believe it and receive it!

SECRET # 2—A confident woman refuses to live in fear.

"I will not fear" is the only acceptable attitude we can have toward fear. That does not mean that we will never *feel* fear, but it does mean that we will not allow it to rule our decisions and actions. The Bible says that God has not given us a spirit of fear (2 Timothy 1:7). Fear is not from God; it is the devil's tool to keep people from enjoying their lives and making progress. Fear causes a person to run, retreat, or shrink back. The Bible says in Hebrews 10:38 that we are to live by faith and not draw back in fear—and if we do draw back in fear, God's soul has no delight in us. That does not mean that God does not love us; it simply means that He is disappointed because He wants us to experience all of the good things He has in His plan for us. We can receive from God only by faith.

We should strive to do everything with a spirit of faith. Faith is confidence in God and a belief that His promises are true. When a person begins to walk in faith, Satan immediately tries to hinder her through many things, including fear. Faith will cause a person to go forward, to try new things, and to be aggressive. I believe fear is the main evil force that Satan uses against people. Fear causes people to bury their talents due to fear of failure, judgment, or criticism. It causes them to draw back in misery and live in torment.

Unless we make a firm decision to "fear not," we will never be free from the power of it. I encourage you to be firm in your resolve to do whatever you need to do, even if you have to "*do it afraid!"* To "do it afraid" means to feel the fear and do what you believe you should do anyway. The only thing we really need to do is fear God, reverentially.

Satan is a liar. He lies to people and places images on the picture screen of their minds that show defeat and embarrassment. For this reason, we need to know God's promises (His Word) so we can cast down the lies of the enemy and refuse to listen to him.

Fear seems to be an epidemic in our society. Are you afraid of anything? Is it rejection, failure, the past, the future, loneliness, driving, aging, the dark, heights, life, or death? The list of fears that people experience can be endless. Satan never runs out of new fears to place in any individual's life. At least not until they firmly make their mind up that they will not live in fear. You can trade in pain and paralysis for power and excitement. Learn to live beyond your feelings. Don't allow feelings of any kind to dominate you, but instead remember that feelings are fickle. They are ever-changing. The bad ones are there when you wish they weren't, and the good ones disappear when you need them most.

God wants to teach us to walk in the Spirit, not the flesh, and that includes emotions. We cannot walk in the vanity of our own mind, in our feelings or our own will and ever experience victory in our lives. God says, *"Fear not,"* and we must be determined that we will obey Him in this area. Fear may present itself as a feeling but if we refuse to bow down to it—that is all it is . . . a feeling! Think about it: Should you be intimidated by a mere feeling? (The subject of fear will be dealt with extensively later in the book).

SECRET #3—A confident woman is positive.

Confidence and negativity do not go together. They are like oil and water; they simply do not mix. I used to be a very negative woman, but, thank God, I finally learned that being positive is much more fun and fruitful. Being positive or negative is a choice—it is a way of thinking, speaking, and acting. Either one comes from a habit that has been formed in our lives through repetitious behavior. You may be like me. I simply got off to a bad start in life. I grew up in a negative atmosphere around negative people. They were my role models, and I became like them. I really didn't even realize my negative attitude was a problem until I married Dave in 1967. He was very positive and began asking me why I was so negative. I had never really thought about it, but as I began to, I realized that I was always that way. No wonder my life was so negative. I began to understand that I was expecting nothing good—and that is exactly what I got.

People don't enjoy being around an individual who is negative so I often felt rejected—which added to my fears and lack of confidence. Being negative opened the door for a lot of problems and disappointments, which in turn fueled my negativity. It took time for me to change, but I am convinced that if I can change, anybody can. Fear is the dark room where all of your negatives are developed, so why not look at the brighter side of life? Why not believe something good is going to happen to you? If you think you are protecting yourself from being disappointed by not expecting anything good, you are mistaken. You are living in disappointment if you are doing that. Every day is filled with disappointment if all your thoughts and expectations are negative. What is wrong with looking at the sun instead of the clouds? What is wrong with seeing the glass half full instead of half empty?

When encouraged to think positively, people often retort, "That is not reality." But the truth is that positive thinking can change your current reality. God is positive, and that is His reality. It is the way He is, the way He thinks, and the way He encourages us to be. He says that all things can work out for good if we love Him and want His will in our lives (Romans 8:28). He says we should always believe the best of every person (1 Corinthians 13:7).

It has been said that 90% of what we worry about never happens. Why do people assume that being negative is more realistic than being positive? It is a simple matter of whether we want to

look at things from God's perspective or Satan's. Who is doing
your thinking for you? Are you
doing your own thinking, choosing your thoughts carefully or,
are you passively thinking what-

> A person is not a failure because she tried some things that did not work out. She fails only when she stops trying.

ever kind of thoughts that fill your mind? What is the origin of
your thoughts? Are they agreeing with Scripture? If they are not,
then they didn't originate with God.

Thinking negatively makes you miserable. Why be miserable
when you can be happy?

Thinking negatively prevents you from being aggressive, bold,
and confident. Why not think positively and walk with confidence?

SECRET #4—A confident woman recovers from setbacks.

We don't need to see setbacks as failures. A person is not a failure
because she tried some things that did not work out. She fails only
when she stops trying. Most of the people who are huge successes
failed their way to success. Instead of allowing mistakes to stop
you, let them train you. I always say that if I step out and try something and it does not work, at least I know not to do that again.

Many people are confused about what they are to do with their
lives. They don't know what God's will is for them; they are without direction. I felt the same way once, but I discovered my destiny by trying several things. I tried working in the nursery at
church and quickly discovered that I was not called to work with
children. I tried being my pastor's secretary, and after one day I
was fired with no explanation except, "This just isn't right." I was
devastated at first, until a short while later I was asked to start a
weekly meeting on Thursday mornings at church and teach God's
Word. I quickly found where I fit. I could have spent my life being
confused, but I thank God that I was confident enough to step out
and discover what was right for me. I did it through the process of

elimination, and I experienced some disappointments—but it all worked out well in the end.

If you are doing nothing with your life because you are not sure what to do, then I recommend that you pray and begin trying some things. It won't take long before you will feel comfortable with something. It will be a perfect fit for you. Think of it this way: When you go out to buy a new outfit, you probably try on several things until you find what fits right, is comfortable, and looks good on you. Why not try the same thing with discovering your destiny? Obviously there are some things you cannot just "try"— like being an astronaut or the President of the United States—but one thing is for sure: You cannot drive a parked car. Get your life out of "park," and get moving in some direction. I don't suggest going deep in debt to find out if you should own a business, but you could begin in some small way, and, if it works, take it to the next level. As we take steps of faith, our destinies unfold. A confident woman is not afraid to make mistakes, and if she does, she recovers and presses on.

One of the great things about a relationship with God is that He always provides new beginnings. His Word says that His mercy is new every day. Jesus chose disciples who had weaknesses and made mistakes, but He continued working with them and helping them become all that they could be. He will do the same thing for you, if you will let Him. The apostle Paul emphatically said that it was important to let go of what lies behind and press toward the things ahead (Philippians 3:13). Don't be afraid of your past; it has no power over you except what you give it. Not letting the past dictate your future is part of the confident lifestyle.

Recovering from pain or disappointment of any kind is not something that just happens to some people and not to others. It is a decision! You make a decision to let go and go on. You learn from your mistakes. You gather up the fragments and give them to Jesus, and He will make sure that nothing is wasted (John 6:12). You refuse to think about what you have lost, but instead you inventory what you have left and begin using it. Not only can you recover, but you can also be used to help other people recover. Be a living example of a confident woman who always recovers from setbacks no matter how difficult or frequent they are. Don't ever say, "I just cannot go on." Instead, say, "I can do whatever I need to do through Christ who strengthens me. I will never quit, because God is on my side."

SECRET #5—A confident woman avoids comparisons.

Confidence is not possible as long as we compare ourselves with other people. No matter how good we look, how talented or smart we are, or how successful we are, there is always someone that is better, and sooner or later we will run into them. I believe confidence is found in doing the best we can with what we have to work with and not in comparing ourselves with others and competing with them. Our joy should not be found in being better than others, but in being the best we can be. Always struggling to maintain the number-one position is hard work. In fact, it's impossible.

Advertising is often geared to make people strive to look the best, be the best, and own the most. If you buy "this" car, you will really be number one! If you wear "this" particular brand of clothes, people will really admire you! Try "this" new diet and lose those few extra pounds—and then you will be accepted and noticed. The world consistently gives us the impression that we need to be something other than what we are—and that some product or program or prescription can help us do that. Like most people, I struggled for years trying to be like my neighbor, my husband, my pastor's wife, my friend, and so on. My neighbor was very creative at decorating, sewing, and many other things, while I could barely sew a button on and have confidence that it would not fall off. I took lessons and tried to sew, but I hated it.

My husband is very calm and easygoing, and I was just the opposite. So I tried to be like him, and that didn't work either. My pastor's wife was sweet, mercy-motivated, petite, cute, and a blonde. I, on the other hand, was aggressive, bold, loud, not-so-petite— and a brunette (if my hair was colored recently, that is).

In general, I found myself always comparing myself with someone, and in the process rejecting and disapproving of the person God created me to be. After years of misery, I finally understood that God does not make mistakes, He purposely makes all of us different, and different is not bad; it is God showing His creative variety. Psalm 139 teaches us that God intricately formed each of us in our mother's wombs with His own hand and that He wrote all of our days in His book before any of them took shape. As I said, God does not make mistakes, so we should accept ourselves as God's creation and let Him help us be the unique, precious individual that He intended us to be.

Confidence begins with self-acceptance—which is made possible through a strong faith in God's love and plan for our lives. I believe it is insulting to our Maker (God) when we compare ourselves with others and desire to be what they are. Make a decision that you will never again compare yourself with someone else. Appreciate others for what they are and enjoy the wonderful person you are.

One of the Ten Commandments is "Thou shall not covet" (Exodus 20:17). That means we are not to lust after what other people have, how they look, their talents, personality or anything else about them. I believe lust is present when we want something so much that we cannot be happy without it. It is possible to resent someone because he or she has what we don't. These attitudes are not pleasing to God. Another person can be an example to us, but should never be our standard. The Bible says in Romans 8:29 that we are destined to be molded into the image of Jesus Christ and share inwardly His likeness. Another Scripture says that we have the mind of Christ (1 Corinthians 2:16). We can think, speak, and learn to behave as Jesus did, and He certainly did not ever compare Himself with anyone or desire to be anything other than what

His Father had made Him to be. He lived to do the Father's will, not to compete with others and compare Himself to them.

I encourage you to be content with who you are. That does not mean that you cannot make progress and continually improve, but when you allow other people to become a law (rule or regulation), you are continually disappointed. God will never help you be someone else. Remember that being "different" is good; it is not a bad thing. Celebrate your uniqueness and rejoice in the future God has planned for you. Be confident and start enjoying you!

SECRET #6—A confident woman takes action.

I have heard that there are two types of people in the world. The ones who wait for something to happen and the ones who make something happen. Some people are naturally shy, while others are naturally bold, but with God on our side we can live in the supernatural, not the natural. We all have something to overcome. A naturally bold person has to overcome pride, excessive aggression, and false confidence, while the naturally shy must overcome anxiety, timidity, the temptation to withdraw from challenges, and low confidence.

A bold person can often be assertive to the point of being rude. I like bold people who are not afraid of me, but I don't like people who don't respect me and have bad manners. What some people think is boldness is, in reality, pride—which is one of the things God's Word says that He hates. I am naturally bold and have had to stand against pride. It seems that bold people just naturally assume they are right about most things, and they don't mind telling other people just how right they are. And, while confidence is a good thing, egotism is not. Thank God we can learn to have balance in our lives. We can benefit from our strengths and overcome our weaknesses through His help.

A shy person shrinks back from many things that she should confront. There are many things she would like to say or do, but

God works through our faith, not our fear

she's paralyzed by fear. I believe we must learn to step out into things and find out what God has for us in life. A more timid approach may protect individuals from making mistakes, but the result is that they spend their lives wondering "what could have been." Bold people, on the other hand, make more mistakes, but they recover and eventually find what is right and fulfilling for them.

Making mistakes is not the end of the world. We can recover from mistakes. In fact, one of the few mistakes we cannot recover from is the mistake of never being willing to make one in the first place! God works through our faith, not our fear. Don't sit on the sidelines of life wishing you were doing the things you see other people doing. Take action and get a life!

If a person is naturally introverted or extroverted, she will always have greater tendencies toward that natural trait—and that is not wrong. As we have stated previously, God creates all of us differently. However, we can have the life we desire and still not deny who we are. So search your heart and ask yourself what you believe God wants you to do—and then do it. Where He guides, He always provides. If God is asking you to step out into something that is uncomfortable for you, I can assure you that when you take the step of faith, you will find Him walking right beside you.

When you want to do something, don't let yourself think about all the things that could go wrong. Be positive and think about the exciting things that can happen. Your attitude makes all the difference in your life. Have a positive, aggressive, take-action attitude, and you will enjoy your life more. It may be difficult at first, but it will be worth it in the end.

I actually believe it is more difficult for a bold person to overcome pride than it is for a shy person to overcome timidity. If you are shy and timid, just remember it could be worse. Make a decision that with God's help you will be the person He intended you to be and you will have the life He wants you to have.

God Honors Faith

Faith honors God and God honors faith! A story from the life of missionaries Robert and Mary Moffat illustrates this truth. For ten years, this couple labored in Bechuanaland (now called Botswana) without one ray of encouragement to light their way. They could not report a single convert. Finally, the directors of their mission board began to question the wisdom of continuing the work. The thought of leaving their post, however, brought great grief to this devoted couple, for they felt sure that God was in their labors, and that they would see people turn to Christ in due season.

They stayed; and for a year or two longer, darkness reigned. Then one day a friend in England sent word to the Moffats that he wanted to mail them a gift and asked what they would like. Trusting that, in time, the Lord would bless their work, Mrs. Moffat replied, "Send us a communion set; I am sure it will soon be needed." God honored that dear woman's faith. The Holy Spirit moved upon the hearts of the villagers, and soon a little group of six converts united to form the first Christian church in that land. The communion set from England was delayed in the mail; but on the day before the first commemoration of the Lord's Supper in Bechuanaland, the set arrived.[1]

SECRET #7—A confident woman does not live in "if only," and "what if."

The world is filled with people who feel empty and unfulfilled because they have spent their lives bemoaning what they did not have, instead of using what they do have. Don't live in the tyranny of "if only." If only I had more education, more money, more opportunity or someone to help me. If only I had a better start in life;

if only I had not been abused; if only I were taller. If only I weren't *so* tall. If only, if only, if only. . . .

One of the biggest mistakes we can make in life is to stare at what we don't have or have lost and fail to take an inventory of what we do have. When Jesus desired to feed 5,000 men—plus women and children—the disciples said all they had was a little boy's lunch, which consisted of five small loaves of bread and two fish. They assured Him it was not enough for a crowd the size they had. However, Jesus took the lunch and multiplied it. He fed thousands of men, women, and children and had twelve baskets' worth of leftovers (Matthew 14:15–21). The lesson for us: If we will just give God what we have, He will use it and give us back more than we had to begin with. The Bible says that God created everything we see out of "things that are unseen," so I have decided that if He can do that, surely He can do something with my little bit—no matter how unimpressive it is.

When God called Moses to lead the Israelites out of Egypt, Moses felt very inadequate and kept telling God what he could not do and did not have. God asked him what he had in his hand and Moses replied, "A rod." It was an ordinary rod, used for herding sheep. God told him to throw it down, implying that Moses was to give it to Him. When God gave the rod back to Moses, it was filled with miracle-working power and was used by Moses to part the Red Sea as well as other miracles. I repeat, if you will give God what you have, no matter how little and ineffective you may think it is, God will use it and give you back more than you gave Him.

In other words, it is not our abilities that God desires, but it is our availability He wants. He wants us to see possibilities, not problems. Don't spend your life thinking "if only" you had something else, then you could do something worthwhile. "If only" is a thief of what could be.

"What if" can be just as devastating as "if only"—if the what-if is applied in a negative manner. Negatively anticipating a future experience is potentially more devastating than actually experiencing the problem.

Consider my friend Heather. One day, she sat in a coffee shop with tears in her eyes. Although she had many skills and was attractive, she lived in fear and allowed it to steal her life. She was miserable most of the time, because fear brings torment. God did not intend us to live in fear and dread. With Heather, there was always something new to be afraid of. This particular time, as we talked, she lamented over the fact that her mother and aunt had died with heart disease—and now she was afraid she would have the same fate. She had three small children and was fearful she would not get to see them grow up. I asked her if she had experienced any symptoms that made her think she was having heart problems. She said she had a tight feeling in her chest. She shared that she had been to the doctor, and after running appropriate tests, he told her she was experiencing symptoms of stress induced by her fear of getting heart disease.

I encouraged her with several Scriptures about living in faith rather than fear, but she persisted in saying "What if I die and my husband is left with the kids?"

I must admit that my patience with Heather was growing short—not because I had no empathy for her, but because the last time we were together she had the same attitude, but a different set of problems. That time it was fear about a new job her husband had started—which would require his being away from home on business trips. She said, "what if" he meets someone else and gets involved with her while he is on the road? She said, "if only" this new job didn't involve travel.

Heather created her own problems by living in "if only" and "what if." Anyone could be miserable with that kind of thinking. She needed to choose to think differently. She had a stronghold of fear in her mind, which probably got started in her childhood, but she could renew her mind through studying God's Word and meditating on it. Often, people want their problems to vanish, but they are not willing to do what they need to do to help themselves. I had many fears in my life, and they still show up from time to time. But I respond by running to God's Word, which strengthens me to take steps of faith, no matter how I feel.

Where the mind goes, the man follows. If you pay more attention to your thoughts and choose to think on things that will help you instead of hinder you, it will release God's power to help you be the confident woman God wants you to be. Think confident and you will be confident!

These seven secrets will help you on your way to being fully confident. There is still a great deal to learn, but these tips are a good beginning.

Chapter Five

THE WOMAN I DID NOT LIKE

Who can compete with the woman described in Proverbs 31? This woman can do it all; she's a great wife, mother, she manages the house, she runs a business, she cooks, she sews—what she doesn't seem to do is get tired! She seems absolutely perfect. Maybe that's why my first response to reading about her was, "I don't like you." Have you ever felt that way after reading this passage? Her lifestyle challenged me in so many areas that I just preferred to not know her at all. At least, that was my attitude thirty years ago when I first started studying my Bible seriously.

The woman in question is such a famous confident woman and yet her name is not mentioned. I am certain this is because God wants each woman to be able to insert her name in this woman's story. I want you to read about her too and then I will share some practical insight that I believe will help you become the confident woman you want to be.

Proverbs 31:10–31

10 A capable, intelligent, and [a] virtuous woman—who is he who can find her? She is far more precious than jewels and her value is far above rubies or pearls.

11 The heart of her husband trusts in her confidently and relies on and believes in her securely, so that he has no lack of [honest] gain or need of [dishonest] spoil.

12 She comforts, encourages, and does him only good as long as there is life within her.

13 She seeks out wool and flax and works with willing hands [to develop it].

14 She is like the merchant ships loaded with foodstuffs; she brings her household's food from a far [country].

15 She rises while it is yet night and gets [spiritual] food for her household and assigns her maids their tasks.

16 She considers a [new] field before she buys or accepts it [expanding prudently and not courting neglect of her present duties by assuming other duties]; with her savings [of time and strength] she plants fruitful vines in her vineyard. [S. of Sol. 8:12.]

17 She girds herself with strength [spiritual, mental, and physical fitness for her God-given task] and makes her arms strong and firm.

18 She tastes and sees that her gain from work [with and for God] is good; her lamp goes not out, but it burns on continually through the night [of trouble, privation, or sorrow, warning away fear, doubt, and distrust].

19 She lays her hands to the spindle, and her hands hold the distaff.

20 She opens her hand to the poor, yes, she reaches out her filled hands to the needy [whether in body, mind, or spirit].

21 She fears not the snow for her family, for all her household are doubly clothed in scarlet.

22 She makes for herself coverlets, cushions, and rugs of tapestry. Her clothing is of linen, pure and fine, and of purple [such as that of which the clothing of the priests and the hallowed cloths of the temple were made].

23 Her husband is known in the [city's] gates, when he sits among the elders of the land.

24 She makes fine linen garments and leads others to buy them; she delivers to the merchants girdles [or sashes that free one up for service].

25 Strength and dignity are her clothing and her position is strong and secure; she rejoices over the future [the latter day or time to come, knowing that she and her family are in readiness for it]!

26 She opens her mouth in skillful and godly Wisdom, and on her tongue is the law of kindness [giving counsel and instruction].

27 She looks well to how things go in her household, and the bread of idleness (gossip, discontent, and self-pity) she will not eat.

28 Her children rise up and call her blessed (happy, fortunate, and to be envied); and her husband boasts of and praises her, [saying],

29 Many daughters have done virtuously, nobly, and well [with the strength of character that is steadfast in goodness], but you excel them all.

30 Charm and grace are deceptive, and beauty is vain [because it is not lasting], but a woman who reverently and worshipfully fears the Lord, she shall be praised!

31 Give her of the fruit of her hands, and let her own works praise her in the gates [of the city]!

I hope you took time to read the verses above. Let's go deeper and examine this passage verse by verse so we can take a good look at each quality this woman represents.

Verse 10

A good woman is hard to find; she is to be valued above rubies or pearls. Good women are precious, more precious than jewels or expensive gems. We must intentionally work to build up our husbands with thoughtful, caring questions and statements because like this verse points out, a woman who is capable, intelligent and virtuous is a rare combination. Any man who has a wife like this should appreciate and value her tremendously.

There are other verses in Proverbs that make it clear how important our role as a woman can be to our role as a wife. A good woman is the crowning joy of her husband but a bad one is like rottenness to his bones (Proverbs 12:4). A wise, understanding and prudent wife is a gift from the Lord (Proverbs 19:14).

Verse 11

Trust is the glue that holds a marriage together and the Bible says that the husband of our Proverbs 31 woman can trust her confidently; he relies on her and believes in her securely. What a blessed thing to be able to say! We live in a society where so many relationships lack these qualities, so when they are present, they should be valued above all else. Confidence, trust and security bring peace and rest to our souls. When we trust others and they trust us, it increases our confidence level. I have confidence in my husband; I trust and feel secure in him. I enjoy these qualities in him and I believe he can also say the same of me. He could not always say that about me. There was a time in my life when I was very unstable but thank God He changes us as we study His Word. We can rely on the promise found in 2 Corinthians 3:18—that if we will continue in God's Word, we will be transformed (changed) into His image from one degree of glory to another. This transformation does not take place all at once but little by little we are changed.

I disliked the woman in Proverbs 31 until I realized she was an example to me, a goal I could reach for. One that God Himself would help me realize if I put my trust in Him and was willing to change. Over a period of many years this woman I once disliked immensely has become a good friend. Quite often when I make decisions I go to her to see what I believe she would do in a similar situation.

Verse 12

This woman comforts her husband and does him good as long as there is life in her. Many marriages could be saved from divorce if a woman would take the initiative to begin comforting and complimenting her husband. The husband also has the same responsibility but if he is not doing it, I encourage you to be willing to step out and be the first to make a move in the right direction for your marriage. We notice in our reading of Proverbs 31:10–31 that there is no mention of what the husband does other than the fact that he praises her and is well known in the city because of his fine wife. I believe if you take the first steps of obedience that God will also deal with your husband and you will see positive changes in him. I also believe it will increase your own level of confidence. When we compliment others we begin to see ourselves in a better light also.

A spiritually mature woman will be the first to do what is right even if nobody else is doing so. We live for God and not for man. We live to please the Lord and not people.

> *Whatever may be your task, work at it heartily [from the soul] as [something done] for the Lord and not for men,*
> *Knowing [with all certainty] that it is from the Lord [and not from men] that you will receive the inheritance which is your [real] reward. [The One Whom] you are actually serving [is] the Lord Christ [the Messiah].* (Colossians 3:23, 24)

Look at the verses just before the passage quoted above (Colossians 3:18–22) and we find instructions for daily living, such as:

> *Wives, be subject to your husbands, [subordinate and adapt yourself to them], as is right and fitting and your proper duty in the Lord.*
> *Husbands, love your wives [be affectionate and sympathetic with them] and do not be harsh or bitter or resentful toward them.*
> *Children, obey your parents in everything, for this is pleasing to the Lord.*
> *Fathers, do not provoke or irritate or fret your children [do not be hard on them or harass them], lest they become discouraged and sullen and morose and feel inferior and frustrated. [Do not break their spirit.]*
> *Servants, obey in everything those who are your earthly masters, not only when their eyes are on you as pleasers of men, but in simplicity of purpose [with all your heart] because of your reverence for the Lord and as a sincere expression of your devotion to Him.*

Please notice that there is an instruction to each group of people in a family household and each one is to obey as something

Verse 13

Our Proverbs 31 woman is not lazy, nor does she procrastinate. She *seeks* (craves, pursues and goes after with all her might) wool and flax and works with willing hands (to develop it). One thing is for sure, whether she is making her family's clothing or making things to sell at the market, she is definitely enthusiastic about it! She does not consider her work drudgery, nor is it something she dreads and complains about doing. This is part of her ministry to her family and she does it with zeal and a positive attitude.

done for the Lord and not for man. If everyone would obey these instructions, think of the peace and joy that would fill each of our homes. There would be no divorce.

Notice too that there is no mention at all of one member only doing what is right if the others do. No, each member is responsible for their part. Each of us will stand before God and give an account of our lives (Romans 14:12). We will not be asked about another person, but only ourselves. Each of us should strive to do the right thing even if we are the only one willing to do so. This greatly honors God and will be rewarded in due time.

Verse 14

She plans good meals that include a lot of variety. She even imports things from far countries to make sure her family does not become bored with eating the same things over and over.

Wow! I'm impressed! I fed my family hamburger 1,001 different ways. I must admit I wasn't too creative. Our budget was meager and I used that as an excuse, but once again our lady in Proverbs challenges us to go the extra mile and make things as good as possible. Making the effort to do things with excellence always makes me feel better about myself and increases my confidence.

Verse 15

She rises before daylight to spend time with God. She knows that she can never be a good wife or mother unless she feeds herself with spiritual food. I am sure she read God's Word, prayed, worshipped and praised and made sure she was spiritually ready for the day.

She also had a plan for the day. This is so important because I don't believe we should be vague and thoughtless, merely getting up daily and waiting to see what happens. People who have this mentality rarely ever accomplish anything, they are usually frustrated and unfulfilled. Have a plan and work your plan. Be disciplined to your plan unless God shows you something else He wants you to do. Our plan does not need to become law, but we should have direction and purpose each day of our lives.

Our Proverbs woman had household help and I am sure many are thinking right about now, "Well, if I had maids I could get something done too." Be careful not to use that for an excuse.

I once knew a woman quite well who was in full-time ministry along with her husband. She was always bemoaning the fact that God had not provided her with any household help. She felt she needed a nanny and a housekeeper, neither of which she had. The more I was around this woman, the more I realized that God had not answered her prayer because she was lazy, disorganized and forever starting things and never finishing them. She needed to show herself faithful in the small things before God would provide the help she thought she needed. She blamed her disorganization and inability to finish projects on the fact that she had no help but that wasn't really the reason. She could have done fewer things and done them well and then God would have enabled her to do more by giving her help. If we do what we can do, God will always do what we cannot do.

> Have a plan and work your plan. Be disciplined to your plan unless God shows you something else He wants you to do.

The majority of women may never have a maid, but there are ways to get our work done and done well. We can enlist the help of children who are old enough to help. We can cut some things out of our schedules that are not really bearing good fruit in order to provide more time for the things we really need to do. I want to encourage you to take charge of your life. Don't let life manage you, you manage it! Decide what you want to do and then do it. Be careful about making excuses, they rob people of their destiny more than any other thing. A great confidence booster is to feel that you are doing with your life what you know you should be doing, rather than wasting it being disorganized and vague.

Consider the Scriptures below:

> Look carefully then how you walk! Live purposefully and worthily and accurately, not as the unwise and witless, but as wise [sensible, intelligent people].
>
> Making the very most of the time [buying up each opportunity], because the days are evil.
>
> Therefore do not be vague and thoughtless and foolish, but understanding and firmly grasping what the will of the Lord is.
> (Ephesians 5:14–17)

Verse 16

This verse is very important to me. I am an aggressive person who wants to be involved in everything but I have learned the hard way that it isn't wise or even possible. We cannot do everything and do anything well. Quality is much better than quantity. Our woman in Proverbs seems to be quite a good businesswoman in addition to being a great wife and mother. Verse 16 begins by saying she "considers" a new field before she buys it. She considers her present duties and is careful not to neglect them by taking on new ones. In other words, she seriously thinks about what she is about to do and does not act emotionally without forethought.

Oh, how much better life would be if we all took time to think about what we are about to do before we do it. It is amazing how many things I don't buy if I just go home and think about it for a while. It is amazing how one good night's sleep changes our minds. The things we thought we had to have yesterday may not even interest us the next day. This shows the fickleness of emotions. They are not all bad, they have the ability to bring pleasure, but they cannot be counted on to be stable. Emotions are fickle and ever changing. This is the reason why it is dangerous to do things based on high emotions without giving plenty of consideration to everything involved.

By not moving emotionally the Bible says the woman saves time and strength which she then uses to plant fruitful vines in her vineyard.

Everything that looks good is not good and a wise person will take time to examine things thoroughly. If you think about it, what is good is sometimes the enemy of what is best. There may be lots of good opportunities for you to minister in your church; but that doesn't mean that each opportunity is the best choice for you.

We should choose the more excellent things and not merely settle for another good thing. I receive many good opportunities almost daily and I have to decline to be involved in most of them. I know what I am called by God to do and I stick with my call.

Here is an example: I was recently traveling outside the United States and at the last moment, after my schedule was already set, I received an invitation to speak to the Senate of that nation. My staff encouraged me to take the opportunity but something did not feel right inside my heart about it. I took my time to answer and by not moving too fast and saying yes to something I really had no enthusiasm about, God dropped a question in my heart to ask. I asked if the entire Senate would be required to be there or if it would be voluntary attendance only. The answer came back that the Senate was not in session and that it would be voluntary.

They also explained that they might have two people or five and the total speaking time would be for five minutes. I don't make light of five minutes or two people, but when considered with the other things I had an opportunity to do that day I knew I had to say no. I encourage you to take time to think about things. He who is hasty almost always ends up unhappy.

Our woman in Proverbs 31 expanded prudently. She was in fact a prudent woman and prudence means good management of resources. Each of us has an allotted amount of time and energy and we should manage it in such a way that we bear the most fruit we can. Emotionally driven people usually lead frustrated lives. They are filled with creative ideas but are unable to settle down long enough to lay out a blueprint and get a solid foundation. They want instant results and if they don't get them they are usually off to another new project that will also fail.

Any time you want to end up with a quality product, business, ministry or marriage it will take time and patience. Dave and I now enjoy an international ministry that is helping millions of people, but it took thirty years to build.

I encourage you to "consider" decisions, purchases, and life choices. Be sure you expand prudently. Don't court neglect of other duties by taking on new ones, unless of course those present duties can be moved on to someone else to make room for your new venture. A sure way to lose your confidence is to have so much to do that you are not doing any of it well.

Verse 17

Our friend in Proverbs 31 even exercises! Verse 17 begins by saying she girds herself with spiritual and mental strength. We know from a previous verse that she prepared herself spiritually for the day. Perhaps she gains mental strength by meditating on God's Word throughout the day. Or she may be an avid reader. Perhaps she stays informed of current events so she can converse intelligently with just about anyone. She remains physically fit for her God-given task which can only mean that she gets plenty of exercise. It may be through her work or something she sets aside time for but she stays physically fit.

I became so concerned about the conditions that most people let their body get into that I wrote a book which was released in April 2006 titled *Look Great, Feel Great: 12 Keys to Enjoying a Healthy Life Now!* As a Christian, your body is the temple of the Holy Spirit and you need to keep it in good condition so God can work through you the way He desires to. Being excessively tired can adversely affect us and our spiritual life. We are not as spiritually sharp as we should be, and it is easier to be deceived. We don't have the desire or stamina to pray as normal. We don't present the best witness to others. It is even easier to be grouchy and unable to walk in the fruit of the Spirit when we feel tired most of the time.

I encourage you to make room in your life for exercise. You

might say, "Joyce, I hate to exercise," or "I don't have time to exercise." I'm very familiar with those excuses because they have been mine for most of my life. I am not where I need to be yet but I am making progress. I have finally decided that, to do what I can do is better than doing nothing at all. Find something you can enjoy and still get exercise. Try walking or playing a sport to get the exercise you need. Exercising with other people might work for you. Reading occasionally on the benefits of exercise will motivate you to include it in your life. Remember, without knowledge, people perish.

People who exercise regularly do tend to be more confident. For one thing, they feel better and more energetic so they accomplish more and enjoy what they do. They usually look better and that increases confidence. Exercise also relieves tension and stress which will help anyone's confidence. Don't think about exercising anymore, just do it!

Verse 18

We all have times in life when we feel like giving up and our woman in Proverbs was no different than the rest of us. However, verse 18 begins with an important statement; "she tastes and sees that her gain from work (with and for God) is good." The verse of Scripture goes on to say that her lamp does not go out even in times of trouble, privation or sorrow. She continues on in faith dispelling fear, doubt and distrust.

Taking time to enjoy the fruit of your labors is one of the main things that will help you keep pressing on in difficult times. God gave many men and women in the Bible difficult tasks to perform but He always promised a reward. Looking to the reward helps us endure the difficulty. The Bible says in Hebrews 12:2b that Jesus despised the cross but He endured it for the joy of obtaining the prize that was set before Him. He is now seated at the right hand of the Father.

Think about Abraham's story. This man was asked to leave his relatives and his country and go to a land that he was unfamiliar with. It was a difficult choice to make but God promised that if Abraham would obey he would be blessed and be a blessing to many.

I encourage you not to look merely at your work but look also at the promise of reward. Take time to enjoy the fruit of your labor and you'll be energized to finish your course. It will also build confidence as you realize that you are worth enjoying the reward of your labors and it is indeed God's will for you.

Verse 19

We see our woman working again. She is apparently making clothes for her family or apparel to sell in the market place. One thing is for sure: We don't see her wasting time.

I believe that being fruitful makes one confident. We are not created by God to waste anything He has given us and time is certainly one of the greatest assets we have. Everyone has the same amount of it and yet some do so many things with theirs while others do nothing. You will never experience confidence if you waste your life and your time.

Verse 20

Mrs. Proverbs 31 is a giver. She opens her hands to the poor. She reaches out her filled hands to the needy (whether in body, mind or spirit).

Look at how she takes the initiative in giving. She opens her hands, she reaches out. I believe a true giver looks for opportunities to give; they search them out. Job said "I was a father to the poor and needy; the cause of him I did not know I searched out" (Job 29:16). Job even went so far in chapter 31 to state that if he did not use his arm to help people then someone should break it out of its socket!

In my opinion, givers are powerful people; they are happy and fulfilled. I lived a long, long time as a selfish, self-centered woman and I was miserable all the time. I have learned over the years, though, to be an aggressive giver; I look for opportunities and it makes my life exciting and fulfilling. There is nothing better in the world than making someone else happy. Remember that what you make happen for others, God will make happen for you. Put a smile on someone else's face and your own joy will increase.

Notice that our woman in Proverbs 31 reached out her filled hands to the needy. When a person truly wants to give, God will give seed to sow. Even if you don't have extra money to give, you do have something. Look around your house and start giving away everything that you are not using or wearing. If an article of clothing has been in your closet one year without being moved, there is a good chance you will never wear it again. Pass it on to someone in need and God will bless you with new things as you need them. I believe that we know giving is the right thing to do. In our hearts we can sense joy and confidence when we become givers and not merely takers.

It is no wonder I did not like this woman in Proverbs 31 when I first started reading about her. She was everything I was not but needed to become. When people are doing something better than we are, we shouldn't reject them—we should be smart enough to learn from them! We don't have to compare ourselves with them, but we can learn and let them be an example.

Verse 21

The Bible states that she doesn't fear bad weather because her family is doubly clothed in scarlet. Could this mean that she has made scarlet clothing for them and also covered them in prayer with the blood of the Messiah? A Messiah, who for her, was still yet to come? We see two cross-references in the Bible to this scripture. One verse is Joshua 2:18, which shows Rahab, a woman with a sinful past, displaying a scarlet thread in her window as Jericho is destroyed. When Joshua's men came to spy on Jericho, Rahab helped keep them safe, and as a reward for her efforts, she asked that no harm come to her family. The scarlet thread represented the Savior who was to come, just as the blood placed on the lintel and door posts of the Israelites in Egypt did on the night of Passover (Exodus 12:13).

The second reference is Hebrews 9:19–22 which gives a vivid account of Moses sprinkling the blood of slain calves and goats on the Book of the Law and covenant and on all the people. It was also put on the tabernacle, the appliances and vessels. In fact, under the law almost everything was purified by blood for the release of sin, guilt and punishment due. Thank God we have a much better covenant ratified in the blood of Jesus! Why blood? Life is in the blood and life is the only thing that can conquer death. Sin is merely death in small doses. We all sin and make mistakes but we can be continuously cleansed by the blood of Jesus as we place our faith in Him.

The woman in Proverbs that we are studying was probably well aware of the power of blood. Therefore she covered her family in scarlet garments which may have well represented the blood of the coming Messiah to her.

One of the things you can do as a confident woman is apply the blood of Jesus Christ by faith to your household. I do this regularly. I apply it to my own life, my mind, emotions, will, body, conscience, spirit, finances, relationships, my walk with God, my husband, children and their families, co-workers and all the partners of Joyce Meyer Ministries. I do this by praying and releasing my faith that there is indeed power in the blood of Jesus to cleanse and protect.

Regularly repenting for sin in my life and keeping my conscience covered with the blood of Jesus helps me be more confident before God, in my prayers and daily life. Guilty people don't function well. They are fearful and usually depressed to some degree. You don't have to be guilty and condemned; you can admit your sins, and ask God to forgive you, and to cleanse you in the blood of Jesus. As you place confidence in His Word, your own confidence will increase.

Verse 22

I am particularly fond of verse 22 because it tells me that our famous Proverbs woman had nice things herself. She lived a balanced life. She did a lot for others, but she also took time to minister to herself. Many people burn out because they don't take time to refresh themselves. We feel such a need to give and do for others that we ignore our own needs or worse, we feel guilty for even thinking about ourselves. We need to be ministered to spiritually, mentally, emotionally and physically. Each one of these areas is important to God; He made them and He is interested in the well being of all of them, including our physical and emotional needs. Our confident woman made herself cushions, rugs and clothing. Her clothes were made of the same cloth that the priests wore. In other words, she had really nice stuff. The best!

Many people have the mistaken idea that Christianity means to do for everyone else but sacrifice everything in life you might personally enjoy. I don't believe this! We will certainly be called to times of sacrifice all throughout life and whatever God asks us to give up we should do so gladly. But we don't have to make it a contest to see just how much we can do without in life in order to try to impress and please God. Jesus said, "I came that they might have and enjoy life, and have it in abundance (to the full) till it overflows" (John 10:10).

This woman had nice things and the Bible says she made them for herself. If you are doing nothing for yourself, you need to find out what you enjoy and allow yourself the privilege of ministering to your own needs as well as everyone else's. Obviously, you should not spend money on yourself that you don't have or become excessive in doting on yourself. But giving very little attention, if any, to your own needs is not healthy, nor does it please God.

I believe we feel more confident when we look our best and take good care of ourselves. You are worth being cared for and don't ever forget it. You have value and you should make an investment in yourself.

Verse 23

Our woman has a famous husband but it is because of his fine wife. What a huge compliment to her! Just imagine if your husband went to a party and everyone flocked around him commenting about what a great wife he had. Or, if he were walking down the street and two men on the other side of the street had a conversation that went something like this: "There goes Mr. Proverbs 31, and man, does he have a great wife. You would not believe all this woman accomplishes in life! She not only takes care of everybody else, she takes really good care of herself also. Yes sir, Mr. Proverbs 31 is a blessed man. God's favor is certainly on him to give him such a fine wife."

Make a decision to be the kind of wife that will cause others to believe your husband is blessed because he has you.

Verse 24

Now we find our multi-talented woman making garments to sell in the market place. What a woman—she even adds to the family income by using some of the same skills she needs at home to be a blessing to others. I like the fact that she makes sashes that free one up for service. The clothing style of the culture she lived in required people to gather up their skirts and tie them so they could work unhampered. She made sashes that would do this. It was also something everyone needed. If you are going to go into business, make sure you do enough research to be sure a lot of people will need what you are going to offer.

Verse 25

Proverbs 31:25 tells us that her strength and dignity are her clothing, and her position is strong and secure. This certainly must have increased her confidence. She wasn't afraid of losing her position or something bad happening.

> Knowing you are prepared for whatever comes will increase your confidence in an amazing way.

She boldly faced the future because she knew she and her family were prepared for it. Lack of preparation is one of the major causes for low confidence. (I will dedicate an entire chapter to this later in the book.) Being prepared requires working ahead of time instead of putting things off until the last minute. Matthew 25 tells us of ten virgins. Five were wise and five were foolish. The wise took extra oil with them as they waited for the bridegroom to come but the foolish didn't do anything to prepare. The bridegroom was slow in coming and, sure enough, the foolish ran out of oil. When he did come, they wanted to borrow from the wise who had extra oil. They had to be told that there would not be enough for all of them and they lost their opportunity to meet the bridegroom.

This same scenario happens to many people in life. They procrastinate until it is too late to take advantage of an opportunity that could have been a tremendous blessing to them.

Knowing you are prepared for whatever comes will increase your confidence in an amazing way. If you are one of the people who put things off, don't procrastinate any longer and start getting prepared today!

Verse 26

Our woman in Proverbs 31 knows the importance of words. She opens her mouth in skillful and godly wisdom. The law of kindness is in her tongue. Speaking kindly to other people is a tremendous attribute and one that certainly enhances a godly woman. We all need kindness and I believe we will reap what we sow. If you need kindness shown to you, then show it to other people. Think about what you are going to say before you say it and you will be more likely to speak with wisdom rather than mere emotion. Proverbs 18:20, 21 says that a man will have to be satisfied with the consequences of his words and that the power of life and death are in the tongue. It goes on to say that we will eat the fruit of our words for life or death.

Not only do we have the capability of speaking life or death to other people, we have the same ability in our own lives. We can speak words that build confidence in ourselves and others or we can speak words that destroy confidence. I encourage you to start increasing your own confidence today by what you say. Be especially careful about self-talk. This is the conversation that you have with yourself inside yourself. You actually talk to yourself more than you do to anyone else. Be sure what you are saying is something you want to live with.

Verse 27

Our friend in Proverbs is a responsible woman. She stays alert to how things go in her household, she refuses to be idle and she doesn't waste her time in things like sitting around gossiping or wallowing in self-pity. She is not discontented. She appreciates life and I believe she celebrates it fully each day. Idleness, waste, self-pity, gossip and discontentment are thieves of the great life Jesus died to give you. Don't allow them to rule you. When you maintain a positive attitude you will enjoy more confidence.

Verses 28, 29

She enjoys the praise of her children and husband. They rise up to call her blessed. Her husband says that many daughters have been virtuous and noble but that she exceeds them all. In other words, he says that she is the best wife anyone could ever have. He applauds and celebrates her strength of character and goodness.

One year my birthday happened to be during one of our conferences and my husband Dave stood up and read Proverbs 31 to me in front of a room filled with people. Then my children one by one rose up to say kind and edifying things to me. There is no better feeling than to spend years raising your children, and then have them tell you that they honor you, love you and don't believe they could have had a better mother. Or, to have your husband say you are the best wife in the world. Those comments certainly were confidence boosters for me.

Verses 30, 31

Charm, grace and beauty can be deceptive because it is not lasting, but the woman who reverently and worshipfully fears the Lord shall be praised. She will eat the fruit of her labors and her works will praise her.

Doing what one believes to be right will always increase confidence. You can't go wrong when you keep God as the focus of your life. Follow the example of the Proverbs 31 woman. She gives us tremendous insight in how to be the best and most confident homemaker, wife, and mother we can be.

Chapter Six

OVERCOMING SELF-DOUBT

Put on a coat or a jacket and have someone tie your wrists together. Then try and take off your jacket. It can't be done, can it? That's what happens when you struggle with believing in yourself, when you let fear and self-doubt tie you up in knots. It's pretty much impossible to succeed! Self-doubt and confidence don't work together, they work against each another. Confidence will destroy self-doubt but self-doubt will destroy confidence.

Self-doubt is tormenting. The woman who doubts herself is unstable in everything she does, feels and decides. She lives in confusion most of the time and wrestles with making decisions and sticking with them because she is forever changing her mind just in case she might be wrong. A confident woman is not afraid of being wrong! She realizes she can recover from making a mistake and doesn't allow the fear of making one to imprison her, or tie her up in self-doubt.

In the Bible, James 1:5–8 teaches us that God cannot answer the prayers of a double-minded person. God responds to our faith, not our fears. Self-doubt is fear. Fear that we will make mistakes or do the wrong thing. It often goes beyond being afraid one will do the wrong thing; more often it involves how people feel totally wrong about themselves. They carry a deep-rooted shame and just can't seem to accept themselves or have confidence in their decision-making ability.

Probably right about now you may be thinking, "Well, Joyce, I really can't help how I feel. I wish I felt confident but I just don't." What I am getting ready to say to you may be one of the

We need to believe God's Word more than we believe our feelings.

most important things you have ever heard in your life. YOU DON'T HAVE TO FEEL CONFIDENT TO BE CONFIDENT! To live in victory, each of us must learn to go beyond our feelings. I have learned that I can feel wrong and still choose to do what is right. I have also learned that I don't have to feel confident to present myself in a confident manner.

If I make a decision and believe it is right at the time I make it, I don't have to change my mind later just because I begin to think or feel I might have made a mistake. If God shows me I have made a mistake then I need to change my decision, but I don't have to bow down to every wild thought or feeling that I encounter. When Satan wars against my mind, I can open my mouth and say out loud what God's Word says about me and you can do the same thing. "For in Him, [I] live and move and have [my] being" (Acts 17:28, pronoun substitution mine).

It is not wrong to say good things about yourself. We should say "God's wisdom is in me and I make good decisions." We need to believe God's Word more than we believe our feelings. We have already established in this book that feelings can be very fickle, and they are ever changing and are not to be trusted to help us make decisions in life. Feelings in and of themselves are not evil but they certainly can and do lead people astray. Feelings are capable of giving us right information but they are also capable of not giving accurate information; therefore, we have to live deeper than emotions. God's Word teaches us to pursue peace (Psalm 34:14, 2 Timothy 2:22, Hebrews 12:14, 1 Peter 3:11).

I have had times in life when I felt peace in my heart about a direction I was taking and yet my head argued with me. James 1:22 clearly teaches us that reasoning leads us into deception and betrayal. When we change our mind about a decision we have made, it should be because we have lost our peace about the direction we intended to take or have gained some wisdom or insight that we did not have previously.

Don't Shrink

Self-doubt causes a person to shrink back in fear. God's Word states in Hebrews that the just shall live by faith and if he shrinks back in fear, God's soul has no delight in him (Hebrews 10:38). That does not mean God is angry with us, but it does sadden Him that we are living so far below the confident life He provided through Jesus Christ.

Faith is being confident in God and His Word. Perhaps you have a good relationship with God and have no problem trusting Him, but when it comes to trusting yourself to do the right thing, you shrink—you allow fear to control you and pull you back.

God once told me that if I didn't trust myself, then I didn't trust Him. He said that He was living in me, and directing, guiding and controlling me because I asked Him to do so. I needed to believe God's promises, not my feelings or thoughts. Of course, any one of us can miss God and we can make mistakes. We can think we are going in the right direction and then discover we are wrong but it's not the end of the world, nor is it anything to become excessively concerned about. If our hearts are sincere and we are honestly seeking God's will, even if we do make a mistake, He will intervene and get us back on track. Quite often, He does it without us even knowing.

I encourage you to believe that you are being led by God unless He shows you otherwise, instead of always assuming you are wrong and living in the agony of self-doubt. Just as God has promised in His Word (John 16:13), trust Him to lead you by His Holy Spirit into all truth. If we are on the wrong track, God will help us get back on the right one.

When Jim Burke became the head of a new products division at Johnson & Johnson, one of his first projects was the development of a children's chest rub. The product failed miserably, and Burke expected that he would be fired. When he was called in to see the chairman of the board, however, he was met with a surprising reception.

"Are you the one who just cost us all that money?" asked Robert Wood Johnson. "Well, I just want to congratulate you. If you are making mistakes, that means you are taking risks, and we won't grow unless you take risks."

Some years later, when Burke himself became chairman of Johnson & Johnson, he continued to spread that word.[1]

Don't be afraid of making mistakes. You will never succeed without making mistakes and possibly many of them. I believe people give their mistakes more power than they need. We should admit them, repent, and ask God to forgive us for them. We should also learn from our mistakes because by doing so, they can add value to our lives. Instead of allowing mistakes to make you feel guilty and bad, let them be your teacher and always remember that just because you make a mistake does not mean you are a mistake.

Learn to separate your "who" from your "do." Making mistakes is something we do as human beings, but we are still God's children and He has a good plan for our lives. He is long-suffering, plenteous in mercy and filled with loving kindness.

Dave and I have four grown children and I can assure you that over the years they have made many mistakes, but they are still my children and I love them just as much as if they had never made the mistakes. Some parents are so protective over their children that they never allow them to make any of their own decisions or mistakes. This is the biggest mistake of all. To grow we must step out and try things. We learn what works and what doesn't. Learning from first-hand experience is a much better teacher than a textbook.

Removing the Sin of Doubt

Self-doubt is simply the fear of being wrong. The Spirit you have received is not a spirit of slavery to put you once more in bondage to fear (Romans 8:15). God does not want you to live in fear, doubting yourself or doubting Him.

If you think about it, doubt is actually sin because in Romans 14:23 the Bible says that "whatever is not of faith is sin." When we allow doubt and despair and fear to take over, that's when the wall to God's blessings starts going up. Don't let that wall even begin to build in your life.

Doubt is a fear of negative things happening, but faith expects good things to take place. It actually takes less emotional energy to walk in faith than in doubt and fear.

People who believe and are positive are much healthier than those who are filled with fear, doubt and negativity. Positive people age slower than negative ones and in fact can live longer.[2]

You may have developed negativity because of various disappointing events in your life but you were never created by God to be negative, fearful and doubtful.

As I have shared, I grew up in a very dysfunctional home. My father was an alcoholic with an explosive temper. He was almost impossible to please. He was physically abusive to my mother and sexually, mentally, emotionally and physically abusive toward me. I experienced many disappointments and devastations by the age of eighteen. I expected bad things to happen, thinking it would protect me from being disappointed when they did. I can honestly say that nothing turned out in my life the way I would have liked for it to at that time.

I left home when I was eighteen, got a job and started trying to take care of myself. I thought I got away from the problem because I physically walked away from it; but I didn't realize I took it with me inside my soul. My mind and emotions were damaged and in need of healing. My will was rebellious and obstinate because I promised myself that nobody would ever hurt me again. My spirit was wounded. I was a broken-hearted person with a very negative attitude. I believed in God and prayed for His help but I knew nothing about the laws of faith. Praying and being negative won't bring an answer. Praying and living in fear won't either. I had much to learn, but over the years God has been faithful, patient and loving. He changed me, healed me, and gave me the opportunity to help other people who are hurting also. He lifted me out of the ash heap and gave me a life worth living.

I am free from fear, negativity and self-doubt. This doesn't mean that these things never try to visit me, but I have learned that I can say "NO" to them just as easy as I can say "YES." When fear knocks on your door, answer with faith. When self-doubt knocks, answer with confidence! When negative thoughts or conversations come up, I am reminded by the Holy Spirit (or sometimes my husband) that being negative will not help anything or anyone and I decide to change.

The Power of Decision

God created each of us with a free will. This gives us the ability to make our own decisions apart from outside influence. Satan tries to force us to do things by placing outside pressure on us but God attempts to lead us by His Holy Spirit from inside our heart where He dwells. Jesus is not demanding or harsh, hard, sharp or pressing. He is humble, gentle, meek and lowly (Matthew 11:29, 30). We are indeed complex creatures. Our mind can think one thing, while our emotions want something else and our will certainly seems to have a mind of its own. Once a person's willpower is renewed by God's Word and they know enough to choose good over evil, they become very dangerous to Satan and his kingdom of

Once a person's willpower is renewed by God's Word and they know enough to choose good over evil, they become very dangerous to Satan and his kingdom of darkness.

darkness. The renewed person can override all the negative things Satan has planned by simply exercising their willpower to agree with God and His Word.

I have discovered that doubt is a thought planted in my head by the devil. He uses it to keep me from enjoying my life and making progress in God's good plan for me. I also have discovered that no matter how doubtful I feel, I can decide to go forward in faith. My feelings are not me. I am greater than my feelings and so are you. No matter how we feel we can still choose to do the right thing. Going against your feelings is not always easy because feelings are frequently very strong, but standing against them until you enjoy freedom is much better than continuing to let them run your life and hold you in bondage.

In Joshua 24:15 we see Joshua make a decision. He says, "Choose you this day whom you will serve, but as for me and my house we will serve the Lord." Joshua made his mind up and nobody was going to change it. He didn't make his decision based on what others did. He refused to live under the fear of man. If you make a decision don't allow yourself to become doubtful just because someone else is not doing what you are doing. Don't assume you are wrong and need to change. Perhaps both of you are right. God leads different people to do different things for reasons that only He knows.

Practice Makes Perfect

I encourage you to practice being a positive person. It's just a matter of breaking one bad habit and forming a new one. I was so negative at one time in my life that if I even tried to think two positive thoughts in succession my brain got into a cramp. But, now I am very positive and actually don't enjoy being with people who are negative.

Discipline is required any time you are forming a new habit. You might consider putting some reminders around your house or in your car. Little signs that say "Be positive." Ask a good friend or spouse to remind you if they hear you slipping into negativism.

Practice trusting yourself rather than doubting yourself. Remember, you could be wrong, but you could also be right so why not take the positive approach first? If you are applying for a promotion at work, don't think to yourself or say, "I probably won't get it." Pray and ask God to give you favor with your employer and then say "I believe I will get the job!" You might ask, "What happens if I don't get it?" But what will happen if you don't try? That's right, absolutely nothing. And if you try and the outcome isn't what you were hoping for, then tell yourself "If the job was right for me, God would give it to me, and since He didn't, He must have something even better in mind for me." You can train yourself to be positive in what appears to be a negative situation. Don't let the devil win! He has spread doubt, fear and negativity since the beginning of time and it is high time we stop allowing him to use us as his vessel.

Expect Favor

God wants to give you favor—kindness that you don't deserve. We see mention of God's favor toward many in the Bible and there's no reason to think He can't offer it to you as well. Learn to believe God for favor. Confess several times a day that you have favor with God and man. You will be amazed at the exciting things that happen to you if you speak God's Word instead of how you feel.

Supernatural favor can be expressed in different ways. You may get the job you want but are not naturally qualified for. People seem to like you for no special reason. You get the best seat in the restaurant with the best waiter. People give you things for no reason at all. Favor means that someone will stop and let you into a line of traffic while others are zooming by as if you are not even there.

Living in God's favor is very exciting. When Joseph was cruelly mistreated by his brothers and they sold him into slavery, God gave him favor everywhere he went. He had favor with Potiphar and was placed in charge of his household. He had favor with the jailer during his imprisonment for a crime he did not commit. He had so much favor with Pharoah that Joseph became second only to Pharoah in power. Yes, God's favor is an exciting way to live. We see so many men and women that we admire in the Bible being given favor. There was Ruth, Esther, Daniel, and Abraham just to name a few. Resist and refuse to let doubt convince you that good things won't happen to you and your family; aggressively expect good things! Ask God to give you divine supernatural favor and then expect to see it in your life, daily.

[What, what would have become of me] had I not believed that I would see the Lord's goodness in the land of the living!

Wait and hope for and expect the Lord; be brave and of good courage and let your heart be stout and enduring. Yes, wait for and hope for and expect the Lord. (Psalm 27:13, 14)

Claim God's Word with Confidence

- "Be strong (confident) and of good courage . . ."—Joshua 1:6
- "He makes my feet like the hinds' [firm and able]; He sets me secure and confident upon the heights." —2 Samuel 22:34
- "And you shall be secure and feel confident because there is hope; yes, you shall search about you, and you shall take your rest in safety." —Job 11:18
- "In peace I will both lie down and sleep, for You, Lord, alone make me dwell in safety and confident trust." —Psalm 4:8

- "By [the help of] God I will praise His word; on God I lean, rely, and confidently put my trust; I will not fear. What can man, who is flesh, do to me?" —Psalm 56:4

It Begins with You

If you have made your mind up that you intend to enjoy the best life God has for you then you must realize that it begins with you. You must believe what God's Word says about you more than you believe what others say or what your feelings or own mind says.

Maybe you had negative messages fed into you since you were a child. It could have been a parent who had troubles themselves and took their frustrations out on you. It could have been a teacher who delighted in belittling you in front of the rest of the class. Perhaps your parents excessively compared you to another sibling giving you the impression that you were flawed. You may have experienced one or more broken relationships and became convinced it was your fault. But, whatever the reason for your self-doubt and negative attitude toward yourself, it has to change if you truly desire to enjoy God's best in your life.

See yourself as God sees you, not the way the world sees you or even the way you see yourself. Study God's Word and you will find out that you are precious, created in your mother's womb by God's own hand. You are not an accident. Even if your parents told you they never really wanted you, I can assure you that God wanted you; otherwise you would not be here on earth. You are valuable, you have worth, you are gifted, you are talented and you have a purpose on this earth. God says that He has called you by your name and that you are His.

Fear not for I have redeemed you [ransomed you by paying a price instead of leaving you captives]; I have called you by your name; you are Mine. (Isaiah 43:1b)

Because you are precious in My sight and honored, and because I love you, I will give men in return for you and peoples in exchange for your life. Fear not, for I am with you . . .
(Isaiah 43:4–5a)

Take a minute and look into your heart. What do you see there? How do you feel about yourself? If your answer does not agree with God's Word, I want to encourage you to begin today renewing your mind about yourself. I have written many books that will help you in this area and of course God's Word is the best reference book that exists.

Not only must we ask God for things He has promised us but we must receive them. John 16:24 says we are to ask and receive that our joy may be full. If you feel unworthy you probably won't ask and even if you do you won't receive by faith. The self-doubt you have will always stand between you and the best God has for you. It is your decision. Don't let feelings rule you anymore. Take a step of faith and start improving your quality of life today. Believe that you make good decisions, that you are a valuable person with a great future and something good is going to happen to you today!

Chapter Seven

THE POWER OF PREPARATION

Preparation equips us to move confidently. Many women lack confidence simply because they are not properly prepared for what they attempt to do. There could be a variety of reasons for this lack of preparation. They don't realize the importance of preparation, they are lazy, or they are too busy doing things that don't help them accomplish their goals and then have no time to do what would help them. Imagine a doctor trying to be confident if he never had any training or preparation. Anyone who is serious about playing a sport always practices and gets prepared. Even as a teacher of God's Word, I never go to the pulpit without being thoroughly prepared. I study, pray and go over and over my notes. Quite often I don't even look at the notes while preaching because by the time I stand up to teach they have become such a part of me that they flow out with ease. Knowing I have done my best to be prepared helps me minister with confidence.

Can you really think of anyone who is an expert at something who does not practice and prepare? I can't. A concert pianist practices, a world class gymnast practices, a dancer practices. All of that practice and preparation builds confidence in the individual.

Moses had a call on his life to deliver the Israelites from bondage where they were being held captive in Egypt. He wanted to get started right away but as he did he killed an Egyptian and was forced to flee from Egypt for many years. Taking action without God's permission showed clearly that Moses was not ready yet. He had zeal but no knowledge. He was emotional, but not prepared. God led him into the wilderness where he remained for forty years being prepared by God for the job ahead of him.

When God gives us a job to do we often think it will be easy to accomplish. However, most things are harder than you ever thought they would be, they take longer than you ever thought you could endure but they also pay greater dividends than you could ever imagine.

When God called me into the ministry I thought it would happen right away. I did not realize that I had a great deal to learn before I would be prepared for the ministry God wanted for me. I spent every free hour I could find studying God's Word and reading books that taught me biblical doctrine and principals. I gave myself to my calling. I started saying no to invitations I received from friends to do things that I felt would just be a waste of time for me. Many of my friends did not understand my new zeal. They actually told me they thought I was going overboard and needed to calm down and return to normal behavior. They thought it was strange that I did not want to run around with them all day as I had in the past going to garage sales, home interior parties, make-up-parties, candle parties, etc. I'm not saying there is anything at all wrong with doing those things, but God was calling me to separate myself and get prepared for a Bible teaching ministry. I could never be a success and glorify God if I was not prepared and preparation takes time and dedication. It really wasn't a sacrifice for me because God gave me an amazingly strong desire to learn, but it was hard for me emotionally to be so misunderstood. I was trying to follow God and my friends got angry and rejected me. I later learned that even that was all part of my preparation.

I taught home Bible studies for five years that consisted of twenty-five or thirty people. I was faithful and received no financial benefits during that time. It was a time of great financial need for Dave and me, but God always provided. Quite often it was last minute and in unexpected ways, but He did provide.

As part of my preparation, God led me to quit my job so I would have some time to prepare. We had three children at the time, plus I was working full time and was quite active in church. It would have been impossible for me to ever have time to prepare had I not sacrificed the salary I made and been willing to trust God for our needs to be met. Learning to trust God in this way was a testing time for me and also part of my preparation for the ministry we now have where we must trust God for literally everything. Trust doesn't just appear in our lives, but it grows as we take steps of faith and experience God's faithfulness.

> Trust doesn't just appear in our lives, but it grows as we take steps of faith and experience God's faithfulness.

Next, I worked under someone else's authority at a church for five years and learned a lot. They were good years, but hard years. Being under authority kept me from doing the things I wanted to do. It was frustrating but definitely a part of God's overall plan for my life and ministry. I always say that people need to learn how to be under authority before they are qualified to be in authority. Being a strong-willed type-A personality made it difficult for me to submit with a good attitude to authority I did not always agree with, but, it was very good for me and part of my preparation.

The third phase of our ministry began in 1985 when God told us to take the ministry and go north, south, east and west. We started holding very small meetings anywhere we could drive to and I do mean small. We rarely ever hosted a meeting of even one hundred people in those days. As of this writing, I have taught God's Word for thirty years. I attended the school of the Holy Spirit. I was prepared, not in conventional ways, but nonetheless prepared by God for the ministry I now enjoy. We travel nationally and internationally. We have offices in thirteen countries and reach approximately two-thirds of the globe by television five days a week. Yes, we have come a long way, but it has taken a long time and a lot of years of preparation prior to each stage of progress.

I have been criticized over the years because I haven't had formal training in a seminary. People have said, "Who are you to be teaching God's Word? Where did you get your credentials?" I am qualified because God anointed me to preach the gospel to the poor and needy (Isaiah 61:1). All we need to do is look at some of the disciples Jesus chose and we quickly see that God does not always or even usually call those who seem to be qualified. The Bible says that He purposely chooses the weak and foolish of the world in order to confound the wise (1 Corinthians 1:26–29).

I can say for sure that God will prepare you in whatever way He chooses. It may be formal training and it may not, but God will use everything in your life to train you if you are willing to be trained. It's sad to say that many people have a great calling on their life but they are too impatient to go through the preparation that is necessary to equip them for the job.

Joseph was a young man with a dream. He dreamed of having authority and being a great man. However, he was young and impetuous and needed some training and preparation. Joseph's brothers hated him because his father favored him and they sold him into slavery. God used the situation as an opportunity to test and train Joseph. He even spent thirteen years in prison for something he didn't do, but whatever happened to Joseph during those years definitely equipped him for his God-ordained role in history. God's favor was on Joseph and he rose to power with only Pharoah himself being greater. He was placed in a position to feed multitudes of people, including his father and brothers during seven years of famine. Your pain can become someone else's gain. Your mess can become your ministry if you will have a positive attitude and decide to let everything you go through prepare you for what is ahead.

Esther had to have a year of preparation before she was allowed to go before the king. For twelve months, she went through the purifying process, but even more than her physical beauty, her inner beauty showed through, and God used her to save her people from wicked Haman's evil plot.

Peter had to be prepared by going through some very humbling experiences; he was a powerful man but a proud man as well. The Lord had to humble him before He could use him. Most strong leaders have a lot of natural talent but they are also full of themselves (pride) and have to learn how to depend on God. They have to trade in their self-confidence for God-confidence. Remember that Jesus said, "Apart from Me you can do nothing" (John 15:5). When He says nothing, He means nothing! We are all like a blade of grass, here today and gone tomorrow. Or, like a vapor or a puff of smoke. We are here and then gone. We dare not think more highly of ourselves than we ought to. We don't want to think too little of ourselves but not too highly either. We just need to see ourselves "in Christ." We are nothing without Him and yet we can do everything with Him.

Don't Try to Wing It

Ever found yourself in a situation where you did not take time to prepare for something at work or at church and you're expected to do something? Your heart starts hammering, the butterflies in your stomach start flittering and you quietly think to yourself, "I'll just wing it." You're not prepared but you're thinking that hopefully you can pull it off anyway and nobody will ever know. Even if you do manage to deceive other people, you will know the truth and you won't feel good about it. Down deep inside you will know that you did not do your best. You might feel relieved that you managed to get through it, but you did it in fear rather than confidence.

Even Jesus was trained and prepared by the suffering He went through. He was literally equipped for His office as High Priest through His times of preparation.

Although He was a Son, He learned [active, special] obedience through what He suffered

And, [His completed experience] making Him perfectly [equipped] He became the Author and Source of salvation to all those who give heed and obey Him. (Hebrews 5:8, 9)

If Jesus needed preparation in order to be equipped for His job, there is no doubt in our minds that we need the same thing.

What Kind of Preparation Do You Need?

As I have already stated, the kind of preparation you need depends on what you are being called to do and your season in life at that time. For many people, schooling is the first type of preparation they get but for others that isn't possible. A married woman with three small children and a part-time job probably could not leave for two years to go to Bible college or to get a degree in business administration. If you do desire schooling and cannot get it full time you might consider taking some evening classes or even Internet classes. Follow your heart and God will lead you to the right destination at the right time.

If you have something in your heart that you believe you are supposed to do but are unable to do it now, don't let that discourage you. We hold some things in our hearts for years before we see them manifest. Let your dream incubate in your heart. Pray about it and do whatever you can to be ready when the time is right.

Our youngest daughter Sandra was in full-time ministry with us for fourteen years and then gave birth to twins. She found it impossible to stay in ministry in the same way during that season of her life. She tried part-time ministry with us and even that didn't work. She was stressed physically and emotionally and was not happy. She realized she had to lay her job down for the season of life she was in but even in this new season, she strongly believes she is still being prepared for the future she has ahead of her. She actually still considers herself to be in ministry because she tries to help and bless people everywhere she goes. It is not as it was, but it is good! It is important that you understand the idea that preparation for what God wants you to do does not have to be formal or conventional training. It is also important that you understand that God does not call everyone into full-time ministry. He may call you into business, government or some other thing, but if you want to do it with confidence you will need preparation.

Even the people who are able to get formal training still need to get some experience. Knowing something in our head and knowing how to apply it practically can be two different things. The Bible says that Jesus gained "experience" through the things He suffered (Hebrews 5:8, 9). God is looking for people with experience in life so ask Him to begin your training and preparation today and you can learn anything you will need for your future. I hate to see young people get out of college and have an "I know it all attitude." We need to be lifetime learners and we can all learn something every day if we let all of life be a school we attend.

In my case, I was not able to go to college when I got out of high school. Due to the abuse in my home I had to get out on my own and begin making a living for myself so I could escape being mistreated. God taught me everywhere I was. I learned some great lessons about integrity, excellence and honesty in the grocery store and shopping malls. At one job I had, I learned how important it is to treat people with kindness when I was treated unkindly myself. Sometimes the bitter experiences we endure are the best teachers we have in life.

I would like to have gone to college. My teachers recognized I had a writing gift and strongly encouraged me to try for a college scholarship in journalism, but all I could think of at that time was getting away from home and into a position where I would no longer be abused. I am happy to say that God gave me more than I could have gotten on my own in the way of college degrees. I have honorary doctorates from Oral Roberts University and Grand Canyon University in Phoenix. I also have two earned degrees based on the seventy-five books I have written and the knowledge contained in them. They include a bachelor's and master's of theology and an earned doctorate of philosophy in theology, all from Life Christian University in Tampa, Florida.

God promises in Isaiah 61:7 to give us a double reward for our former shame and trouble and I am a living witness that His Word is true.

Some people get on-the-job training. They are simply not book people and learn much more quickly by the hands-on method. However we learn, we can be assured that God will prepare us in His own way.

Don't try to put God in a box by thinking that everyone has to do the same thing. Not everyone who serves God in ministry went to seminary or Bible school. Not everyone who is the president or CEO of a major corporation went to college. God equips some people with very strong natural skills and a lot of common sense. Microsoft czar Bill Gates dropped out of Harvard after his freshman year. Instead of going to college, Truett Cathy started a chicken restaurant with strong biblically-based business principles and Chick-fil-A is now the second largest quick service chicken restaurant chain in the country. Our youngest son did not go to college; he is the CEO of our USA office and does a fantastic job. He has God-given gifts and lots of common sense. He sees things and instinctively knows how to handle them. Part of his training came from just being around his father and me for so many years. It is amazing what we learn in life that we don't even realize we are learning until we need to put it into practice.

Our oldest son is the CEO of all the foreign offices and world missions. He had two years of college but none of his schooling had anything to do with what he is doing in life now. He also learned the hard way, by working in every department that existed at *Joyce Meyer Ministries* until he made his way to the top.

I encourage you to let everything in life be preparation for the things you have in your future. Let every experience be something you learn from. Don't despise the days of small beginnings. Those small beginnings are usually all we can handle at the time. God will give more when He knows we are ready. Enjoy every step of your journey. Don't be in such a hurry to rush through things that you miss the lessons you can draw from each day.

Do Your Part and God Will Do the Rest

If you do what you can do then God will do what you cannot do. Do your best to be prepared for the job in front of you and God will come through with some supernatural abilities that will amaze you. I study diligently for my sermons and quite often I hear myself say things when I am teaching that I did not even know that I knew. I did my part and God came through supernaturally with some things to make my message even better. Had I been lazy and thought I did not need to prepare, those supernatural things would not have happened.

To be prepared, you don't have to worry about the part you don't know how to do, just do the part you know. Your faith-filled actions are seeds you sow. Sow your seed in faith and God will bring a harvest at just the right time.

When Jesus ascended to Heaven, He gave gifts unto men (Ephesians 4:8). I am gifted in communication. My worship leader is gifted musically. My two sons are gifted in business administration. My husband is gifted in wisdom and financial management. God has got all the bases covered and we don't have to worry. I want to say once again, "if you will do what you can, then God will do what you cannot do."

If you confidently step out and do your part, God will surround

Insecurity and a lack of confidence will steal the wonderful life that God has planned for you.

you with people who have the gifts and abilities that you don't have. However, when a person lacks confidence, quite often they cannot receive help from other people. They are too busy making comparisons to receive the help God has sent them. Insecurity and a lack of confidence will steal the wonderful life that God has planned for you. It causes us to be jealous of and resent those who we should appreciate.

My husband does not have the same abilities that I do, but he has good abilities. He is confident and does not feel the need to compete with me. We make a good team because we have different abilities. We complement and complete each other. A lot of people never do anything because they cannot do everything. They are negative people who concentrate on what they cannot do instead of seeing what they can do and then do it.

You don't have to be prepared to do the entire job by yourself, just prepare yourself to do the best that you can do and remember that God will add what you don't have.

Know Your Strengths and Weaknesses

So how do you know what you can do and what you cannot do? It's important to understand this if you are to be well-prepared. This will prevent you from wasting your time on something you won't succeed at anyway. I am a good public speaker but I am not a good musician or singer. At one time in my life I decided I wanted to learn to play the guitar. I quickly discovered that I had zero ability in that area. First of all, my fingers are short and do not comfortably reach around the neck of the guitar. I struggled and managed to play a few notes but did not enjoy it at all. Why? Because playing guitar was not what I was supposed to do. Had I continued to insist on learning to play guitar I would have felt like a failure; and had I ever tried to play in front of people I certainly would not have felt confident. As hard as you may try, you cannot be properly prepared and feel confident to do something you are not meant to do.

Make sure that whatever you are trying to do is something you are really meant to do and not just something you want to do to impress people. It is a sad truth that some people spend most of their time and all their money trying to impress people they don't even like.

Don't be afraid to admit what you cannot do. Know your weaknesses and pray for God to send people into your life to do what you cannot do. I cannot sing and play musical instruments but God has always provided me with a good praise and worship leader for my ministry. I don't know anything about all the equipment it takes to record television and air a show worldwide but I am surrounded by people who know what I don't know. I am not afraid to say that I'm not good at something and I don't waste my time trying to develop my weaknesses.

Another very important thing is that you must absolutely know your strengths. Make a list of what you are good at and rehearse it daily until you gain confidence in your abilities. Thinking about what you're good at is not conceited; it is merely preparation to do your job with confidence. I know that anything I am good at is because God has gifted me in that area and I thank Him all the time for the abilities He has equipped me with. Some of you may have never seriously thought about what you're good at and if not it is time for you to begin. Make a list and read it out loud to yourself at least three times a day until you are convinced.

Here's my list:

I am a good communicator
I am a hard worker

I have a lot of common sense
I am organized
I am decisive
I am determined
I am disciplined
I am a loyal friend
I have a good short-term memory
I love to help people
I love to give

I did not make this list in order to brag but to show you how to do it and to encourage you to be bold enough to do it. Make positive affirmations to yourself every day about your qualities. Jesus came to take care of what you could not do so let Him do His job and thank Him for it.

If you are a good mother and homemaker, then say so. I believe I am a good wife and mother. I am not a normal one, but I am a good one. It took me a long time to be willing to say that. For many years the devil convinced me that I was not a good wife and mother because I was not able to do all the things other wives and mothers did. I finally realized that I did not call myself into the ministry, God did. He also gave a grace (special ability) to my family for me to be in ministry. Yes, there were things they had to sacrifice, but there have been benefits also. Each time in life we gain something, we give up something to get it. If you were going to be a concert pianist you would spend many hours practicing while other people entertained themselves and then one day you would have the privilege of being the one who entertained them. You sacrifice and then you reap the seed you have sown.

My entire family sacrificed in order for me to do what I am doing in ministry but we have also had the privilege of helping millions of people worldwide and the joy we get from that has more than made up for anything we gave up.

What are you good at? Do you even know? Have you seriously thought about it or have you been so busy thinking about what you are not good at that you have not even noticed your abilities? Start today reversing the negative flow by being bold enough to actually realize that you are a great person with wonderful abilities. Everyone is! Remember, God does not make junk. After God created the entire world and Adam and Eve, He looked at all of it and said, "It is very good!" In Psalm 139 David describes how God creates us in our mother's womb with his very own hand. How He delicately and intricately forms us. Then he says, "wonderful are your works and that my inner self knows right well." WOW! What a statement. David is basically saying, "I am wonderful and I know that in my heart." He is not bragging on himself, but on God who created him.

The Importance of Prayer

Praying is probably the most important part of preparation, yet so many people today ignore or forget this vital part of the process. I suggest you don't do anything without first praying and asking God to get involved and make it work out right. Jesus said, "Apart from Me you can do nothing," and I believe Him.

The Bible says that we should acknowledge Him in all our ways and He will direct our steps and make them sure (Proverbs 3:6). It's not enough to know that He's there. We must call on Him daily for His guidance and His strength. Think about the young child who insists on putting on a shirt or sweater by himself; he squirms and tugs and twists and groans, and all the while his mom patiently waits beside him, wishing he would ask for help. When Jesus ascended into heaven and sat down at the right hand of the Father, He sent the Holy Spirit to be our Helper in life. He is always ready to get involved, but we must ask for His help. It's like

I have been walking with God most of my life and I am still learning the importance of not trying to do anything without praying.

preparing to cook dinner and a world-renowned gourmet chef walks in and tells you he's available to assist you. The Holy Spirit offers world-renowned supernatural service so why not ask for it? God will enable you to do things that will frequently surprise you if you take Him as your partner in life. But you must start with prayer.

I have been walking with God most of my life and I am still learning the importance of not trying to do anything without praying. The Bible says we are to pray without ceasing. This does not mean that we do nothing all day except pray but it does make the point that prayer is one of the most important things we can ever do. We need to pray our way through the day. Prayer opens the door for God to work in our lives, situations and the lives of our loved ones.

I once heard of a region in Africa where the first converts to Christianity were very diligent about praying. In fact, the believers each had their own special place outside the village where they went to pray in solitude. The villagers reached these "prayer rooms" by using their own private footpaths through the brush. When grass began to grow over one of these trails, it was evident that the person to whom it belonged was not praying very much.

Because these new Christians were concerned for each other's spiritual welfare, a unique custom sprang up. Whenever anyone noticed an overgrown "prayer path," he or she would go to the person and lovingly warn, "Friend, there's grass on your path!" [1]

Prayer makes tremendous power available (James 5:16). Don't let your prayer life reflect weeds of inconsistency or neglect. New confidence can quickly form when you have the power of God's Holy Spirit working in your life. Don't live in weakness when power is just a prayer away.

Prepare for Promotion

Over the years we have released several great people from the ministry simply because we outgrew them. Professionally they were very valuable at one time but they did not continue getting training, even when we offered it to them, so they could go into the future with us. Perhaps some of them were not supposed to stay with us. God probably had something else for them to do. Not everything lasts forever; some things are only meant for a season in life. However, I do believe that some of our former employees missed a great opportunity because they wanted promotion but they were not willing to prepare, they were not willing to take the additional training or learn new skills to help them improve.

It seems like people want more for less these days. There's an entire generation now in their twenties called the "Entitlement Generation," also known as the Millennials, the older end of the generation born between 1979 and 1994. This is a generation that's used to instant gratification and they expect more than they're necessarily willing to work to achieve.[2]

You don't deserve a promotion and a big pay raise just because you sit in a company chair for another year. You must be willing to be more valuable to your employer and the only way you can do that is by taking more responsibility or doing the job you do better than you have done it in the past. Some people get passed over when the company is looking for someone to promote and they never realize it is because they don't do their part to get prepared.

It has always amazed me how some people will be aggressive and do whatever they need to do to be all they can be in life, while others do nothing but complain because nobody is dropping opportunities in their lap. If you want to keep your job then make a decision to grow with your company; don't sit idly by and let it outgrow you.

As I said, "Be a lifetime learner." Read, listen and learn. Go to school or take special classes to keep up with advancing technology in your field. If you make an investment you will reap a reward. The more you know about what you are doing, the more confidence you will have. The more confidence you have, the more confidence others will be able to place in you. Preparation is the key to success. If you get prepared now, you will be promoted later.

Chapter Eight

WHEN THE WORLD SAYS NO

Henry Ward Beecher was a young boy in school when he learned a lesson in self-confidence which he never forgot. He was called upon to recite in front of the class. He had hardly begun when the teacher interrupted with an emphatic, "No!" He started over and again the teacher thundered, "NO!" Humiliated, Henry sat down.

The next boy rose to recite and had just begun when the teacher shouted, "No!" This student, however, kept on with the recitation until he completed it. As he sat down, the teacher responded, "Very good!"

Henry was irritated. "I recited just as he did," he complained to the teacher. But the instructor replied, "It is not enough to know your lesson, you must be sure. When you allowed me to stop you, it meant that you were uncertain. If the entire world says, 'No!' it is your business to say, 'Yes!' and prove it."

The world says, "No!" in a thousand ways:

"No! You can't do that."
"No! You are wrong."
"No! You are too old."
"No! You are too young."
"No! You are too weak."
"No! It will never work."
"No! You don't have the education."
"No! You don't have the background."

"No! You don't have the money."

"No! It can't be done."

And each "No!" you hear has the potential to erode your confidence bit by bit until you quit altogether.

The world might even say, "No! You can't do that, you're a woman." That is what I heard when God called me into the ministry. But I'm not the first woman to be told that I should ignore God's leading on my life or was offered suggestions that conflict with my primary purpose or desire of serving God. As I mentioned in an earlier chapter, the war between women and Satan got its start in the Garden of Eden and has not stopped. Satan hates women because it was a woman who gave birth to Jesus and it is Jesus who has defeated Satan. However, don't think that just because the devil is against you that success is out of your reach. The devil may be against you, but God is for you and with Him on your side you absolutely cannot lose. You just need to be bold enough to say "Yes!" when the world says, "No!"

I remember how hard it was for me to go forward when I stepped out in faith to do what I believed God had called me to do. Most of my family and almost all of my friends turned against me. At that time I didn't really understand the Scriptures that people tried to use against me but I knew that I literally felt compelled to serve God. I had such zeal and desire that it motivated me to go on even when the whole world (with the exception of a few people) was against me. Thank God my husband was for me. His encouragement in those early days was very valuable to me.

Even though most of the world told me I could not do it, I have been doing it for over thirty years and intend to continue until Jesus calls me out of this world. God has done it in spite of what everyone thought. People cannot stop God!

Beware of Being a People-Pleaser

Anyone who tries to keep all the people happy all the time will never fulfill their destiny. Consider the story of the woman from California who kept two bottled water coolers in her kitchen. It wasn't because she was extra thirsty or on a health kick; it was because she couldn't say no to either water company when they called! She was afraid that the salesmen would say bad things about her if she said no.[1]

Maybe you don't have problems saying "no" to telemarketers but maybe you do struggle with saying "no" to your friends, or your family, or your church family, even at the detriment of what you feel God is calling you to do. People are not always happy for your success and even well-meaning people will try to stop you from making progress. You must know your own heart and what you believe you are supposed to be doing and do it. If you make a mistake you will know it soon enough; when you do, don't be too proud to say, "I was wrong."

"Step out and find out," is my slogan. I hate to see people shrink back in fear and be so afraid of making a mistake that they never try to do anything. I know a young man who quit a good job to go into music ministry. It was a bold step and he did everything he could to make it work but it just didn't (at least not at this time). However, I am proud of him that he was bold enough to try. At least now he won't spend the rest of his life wondering what could have been if only he had tried. I think it is better to try and fail than never to try at all. Sometimes the only way we can discover what we are supposed to do with our lives is to try different things until we see what works and what fits right in our heart.

People give us all kinds of advice, most of which we do not ask for. Listen, and as one minister said, "Eat the hay and spit out the sticks." Take anything that is helpful and good but don't let the opinions of other people control you, because as Henry Bayard Swope said: "I cannot give you the formula for success but I can

God uses men and women who are set on obeying and pleasing Him, not those who are controlled by the fear of man.

give you the formula for failure, which is: Try to please everybody."

The Apostle Paul made it clear that if he had tried to be popular with people he would not have been an apostle of Jesus Christ (Galatians 1:10). King Saul lost the kingdom because he allowed his fear of man to cause him to disobey God (1 Samuel 13:8–14). God took the kingdom away from Saul and gave it to David, a man after His own heart. David did not let people control him as Saul did. David's own brother Eliab showed disapproval of him but the Bible says that David turned away from Eliab and continued on with what he was supposed to do (1 Samuel 17:28–30). We should turn away from the people who try to discourage or accuse us instead of allowing what they say or think to affect us adversely.

God uses men and women who are set on obeying and pleasing Him, not those who are controlled by the fear of man. We all want to be liked and accepted but we cannot let that desire control us.

I cover this subject in great detail in my book *Approval Addiction* which came out in 2005; it is a complete guide to overcoming an off-balance need to please people and I wrote it because for years, I tried to be my idea of the perfect Christian, trying to please everyone and pleasing no one and I struggled and suffered for it. Unless you listen to God and follow your own heart you will live an unfulfilled and frustrated life. Anyone who allows other people to control them and guide their destiny will eventually become bitter and feel used and taken advantage of. I am sure you have heard the popular statement, "To thine own heart be true," and I want to say that I highly recommend that if you aren't already doing so, that you start following that advice.

History is filled with people who accomplished great things and yet they had to persevere past the criticism and judgment of people. Some of the world's greatest inventors were persecuted by their family or friends but they pressed on, because they believed in what they were doing.

Benjamin Franklin longed to write for his older brother's newspaper where he worked as a printing apprentice but his brother refused to let him. Ben wrote stories anyway, under a pen name, Silence Dogood, a fictional widow who was very opinionated, particularly on the issue of the treatment of women. Every letter was snuck under the printing shop's door at night to avoid discovery, and "Silence Dogood" became wildly popular. After sixteen letters, Ben finally admitted that he was the writer and though he received quite a bit of positive attention from everyone else, his brother only grew angrier and more jealous. This resulted in Ben receiving beatings and finally running away. Among the many inventions and improvements he created in his lifetime, Ben eventually started his own printing shop and took over a newspaper, the *Pennsylvania Gazette,* which under his supervision became the most successful in the colonies.[2]

After inventing the telephone, Alexander Graham Bell struggled to come up with the money to make his invention a household name. No one really took the invention seriously at first and even his closest family and supporters encouraged him to focus on his improvements to the telegraph instead of that "speaking telephone nonsense." Bankers laughed at him and Western Union initially turned him down. But Alexander refused to give up which is why we have the telephone today.[3]

A Hungarian physician named Ignaz Semmelweis discovered that a deadly infection common in childbirth could be greatly reduced when attendants and doctors thoroughly washed their hands in between patients. Despite lowering the mortality rate of women giving birth, he was laughed out of Vienna for his belief. Still, he wrote down his findings and he is now credited with making childbirth safer.[4]

Margaret Knight worked in a paper bag factory in the mid-1800s when she invented a new machine part that automatically folded and glued paper bags, creating square bottoms instead of the envelope shape that was common at the time. Workmen refused to listen to her advice when installing the equipment because they thought "what does a woman know about machines?" She went on to start the Eastern Paper Bag Company in 1870 and developed more than twenty-six other patented inventions in her lifetime.[5]

Hedy Lamarr is known as a popular movie star from the 1930s and 1940s but she also had an extremely creative and intelligent mind. She earnestly wanted to help with the war effort during World War II and considered leaving acting to join the National Inventors Council but was told her pretty face and star status could do more for the war by encouraging people to buy war bonds. But Hedy never gave up on her dream and helped invent a remote-controlled radio communications system that was patented during World War II and two decades ahead of its time. In addition to her invention that has contributed to multiple technologies used today, she raised millions of dollars to help the war effort.[6]

It has amazed me to read the stories of these men and women who contributed so much to the progress of society in almost every conceivable field and yet they had to endure tremendous criticism, judgment and persecution in order to make something in the world better. This clearly shows how Satan fights progress of any kind. He uses all kinds of fears to try and stop people, but the confident woman will keep pressing on and say "Yes" even when the world screams "No."

What's Wrong with Being Different?

It seems the world opposes, or even fears, anything that is different than the norm. When people are different or they try to do something different, they must be ready for opposition.

Many people who have done great things in life were willing to stand alone and that is not possible without confidence.

Timothy, Paul's "spiritual" son in the ministry, was very young and he was fearful and worried about what people thought of his youth. Paul told him to let no man despise his youth (1 Timothy 4:12). It really does not matter how old or young a person is. If God calls someone to do something and they have the confidence to go forward, nothing can stop them.

The Lord recently spoke to my own heart and said, "Don't ever make decisions based on your age." As Dave and I advanced in age, we found ourselves wondering if we should try new things since we were getting older. God made it very clear that age was not to be the deciding factor. Moses was eighty years old when he left Egypt to lead the Israelites to the Promised Land. At the age of eighty-five, Caleb asked for a mountain to be his property inheritance.

> And now, behold, the Lord has kept me alive, as He said, these forty-five years since the Lord spoke this word to Moses, while the Israelites wandered in the wilderness; and now, behold, I am this day eighty-five years old.
>
> Yet I am as strong today as I was the day Moses sent me; as my strength was then, so is my strength now for war and to go out and to come in.
>
> So now give me this hill country of which the Lord spoke that day. For you heard then how the [giantlike] Anakim were there and that the cities were great and fortified; if the Lord will be with me, I shall drive them out just as the Lord said.
> (Joshua 14:10, 12)

How a person responds to your age and, for that matter, how others respond is really up to you. Of course we all age in years but we don't have to get an "I'm too old" mind-set. Adlai Stevenson said "It is not the years in your life, but the life in your years that counts." Confident people don't think about how old they are,

Celebrate the fact that you're not exactly like everyone else. You are special! You are unique!

they think about what they can accomplish with the time they have left. Remember, confident people are positive and look at what they have, not what they have lost.

Even if you are reading this book and let's say you're sixty-five years old and feel you have wasted most of your life doing nothing but being shy and timid—you can still start today and do something amazing and great with your life.

At the time of this writing my husband, Dave, is 65 and I am 62. We are doing as much now or perhaps even more than ever, but we had to make a decision not to get a "retirement" mentality or to think in terms like, "I'm getting too old for that."

We are determined to let God lead our decision making, not people or our age. I am going to be a confident woman as long as I am on this earth and I know when I go to heaven I will have perfect confidence because there is no fear in God's Presence.

I can say that I am a confident woman because I have decided to be one, not because I always feel confident!

Celebrate the fact that you're not exactly like everyone else. You are special! You are unique! You are the product of 23 chromosomes from your father and 23 from your mother. Scientists say there is only one chance in 10/2,000,000,000 of your parents having another child just like you. The combination of attributes that you have cannot be duplicated. You need to explore the development of your uniqueness and make it a matter of high priority.

It does not increase your value when you find that you can do something that nobody else you know can do, nor does it diminish your value when you are with people who can do things that you cannot do. Our worth is not found in being different or the same as others, it is found in God.

Thousands of years ago the Greek philosopher Aristotle suggested that each human being is bred with a unique set of potentials that yearn to be fulfilled as surely as the acorn yearns to become the oak tree that is within it. I believe thousands upon thousands of people who read this book are people yearning to fulfill a deep longing inside of them. Don't settle for "average" or "getting by." You may have some limitations but you can be extraordinary if you decide to be.

The famous actor Sidney Poitier tells of his life under the colonial system. He shared that in those times the darker your skin was, the less opportunities you could expect to have. His parents, however, and especially his mother cultivated a fierce pride in him that made him refuse to be anything other than extraordinary. They were extremely poor and enough poverty can eventually mess with your mind if you let it, but Sidney kept on believing he could rise above it and he certainly did.[7] Tenacity is a wonderful trait to have. The eagle is tenacious. Once it sets its sights on its prey it will die rather than let go.

Truly confident people are not defeated by opposition; they are actually challenged by it and even more determined to succeed than they were without it.

The world said "No" to Sidney, but he said, "Yes!" What will you say when the world says "No?"

Chapter Nine

ARE WOMEN REALLY THE WEAKER SEX?

One of the misguided ideas about women is that they are weaker than men and that is not true. The Bible says that they are physically weaker (1 Peter 3:7), but it never indicates they are weaker in any other way. Women have the babies and believe me when I say that you cannot be weak and do that.

I might need my husband to open the lid on the new jar of mayonnaise, but I have tremendous endurance when it comes to sticking with something until it is finished. I am not weak and I am not a quitter. As a woman, refuse to see yourself as the "weaker sex."

Don't let that wrong mind-set take hold of you. You can do whatever you need to do in life.

The world is filled with single mothers whose husbands walked out on them and refuse to support their children financially. These moms are giants in my eyes. They work hard and try to be both mom and dad to their children. They sacrifice time, personal pleasures and everything else imaginable because they love their children fiercely. They are certainly not weak.

Men who merely walk away need to remember that strength does not walk away, but it works through situations and takes responsibility.

More than 10 million single mothers today are raising children under the age of eighteen. That number is up drastically from the 3 million reported in 1970 and it's estimated that 34% of families headed by single mothers fall under the poverty line (making less than $15,670 annually).[1] Their biggest concerns are much more basic than many two-parent homes—they worry about affordable, quality child care for their children, keeping a car running and living in a safe, affordable house or apartment.

Some men think that if a woman is a stay-at-home mom and homemaker that she does nothing all day. He may say things like, "I worked all day, what did you do?" These types of comments can make a woman feel devalued, but they are made by men who have a tremendous lack of knowledge. Raising a family, taking care of a man and being a good homemaker is a full-time job that requires overtime with no overtime pay. I applaud the stay-at-home moms, especially those who do their job with joy. You are my heroes!

Going to Bed

Mom and Dad were watching TV when Mom said, "I'm tired, and it's getting late. I think I'll go to bed." She went to the kitchen to make sandwiches for the next day's lunches, rinsed out the dessert bowls, took meat out of the freezer for supper the following evening, checked the cereal box levels, filled the sugar container, put spoons and bowls on the table and started the coffee pot for brewing the next morning. She then put some wet clothes in the dryer, put a load of clothes into the wash, ironed a shirt and sewed on a loose button. She picked up the game pieces left on the table and put the telephone book back into the drawer.

She watered the plants, emptied a wastepaper basket and hung up a towel to dry. She yawned and stretched and headed for the bedroom. She stopped by the desk and wrote a note to the teacher, counted out some cash for the school outing, and pulled a textbook out from under the chair. She signed a birthday card for a friend, addressed and stamped the envelope and wrote a quick list for the supermarket. She put both near her purse.

Mom then creamed her face, put on moisturizer, brushed and

flossed her teeth and trimmed her nails. Hubby called, "I thought you were going to bed." "I'm on my way," she said. She put some water into the dog's bowl and put the cat outside, then made sure the doors were locked. She looked in on each of the children and turned out a bedside lamp, hung up a shirt, threw some dirty socks in the laundry basket, and had a brief conversation with the one child still up doing homework. In her own room, she set the alarm, laid out clothing for the next day, and straightened up the shoe rack. She added three things to her list of things to do for the next day.

About that time, the hubby turned off the TV and announced to no one in particular, "I'm going to bed." And he did.[2]

Men have a lot of wonderful strengths and as we have already stated in this book they have abilities that we don't have, but we are definitely not "the weaker sex."

History Has Not Been Fair

No one could possibly wish to underestimate the influence of women in keeping the home and raising children. Where history has not been "fair" is in failing to record the outstanding achievements of women in areas generally thought to be dominated by men: government, politics, business, religion and science. Men have received credit in these fields but fail to report on the women who have succeeded in them. They seem shocked that a woman could accomplish anything outside the home. This is all part of the record that needs to be set straight. Throughout history, women have accomplished great things.

Let's take a look at ten women who proved everyone wrong. Some of these are well-known and some are not, but all made incredible contributions to the world around them.

Elizabeth I

Wrong gender, great ruler—that about sums up the life of Queen Elizabeth I of England. Her notorious father, King Henry the Eighth, one of the great scoundrels of history, married eight times to father a boy, and accidentally begat a great who was never part of his plans. Elizabeth came to power when her sister Queen Mary, known as "bloody Mary" for her persecution of Protestants, died in 1558. Elizabeth ruled what came to be known as the "Golden Age" of history until 1603.

Elizabeth maintained her rule by pretending to be interested in Catholic suitors so the King of Spain would not invade England. In 1588, King Philip II finally realized he was dealing with a Protestant and sent the great Spanish Armada to conquer England once and for all. Just before this great deliverance for England and as the Armada was approaching, Elizabeth said to her troops at Tillbury, "I know I have the body of a weak and feeble woman, but I have the heart and stomach of a king, and of a king of England too; and think foul scorn that Parma or Spain, or any prince of Europe should dare to invade the borders of my realm." At the end of her reign, she said to her people: "Though God hath raised me high, yet this I count the glory of my crown: that I have reigned with your love."[3]

I love the fact that Queen Elizabeth did not look at her body that she said was frail and weak, but she looked at her heart. She followed her heart and ignored her deficits. God will always strengthen those who are willing to look their weaknesses in the face and say, "You cannot stop me."

Eleanor Roosevelt

Born to a family active in politics but not always progressive when it came to women, Eleanor Roosevelt (1884–1962) received an exclusive boarding school education before she married her distant cousin Franklin Roosevelt in 1905. Over the next few years, with little other than family background, she became the leading woman politician of her day. She had an executive talent that couldn't be denied. With Franklin, she had five children and immediately became active in politics when Roosevelt was elected to the New York Assembly. She worked for the New York State League of Women Voters and the Women's Trade Union League to pass minimum wage laws. When her husband was struck with polio in 1921, she organized Democratic women to help Franklin be elected governor in 1928 and then as president six years later. After her husband's death in 1945, President Truman appointed her as a delegate to the United Nations where she largely shaped the Universal Declaration of Human Rights. Eleanor Roosevelt said: "You gain strength, courage and confidence by every experience in which you really stop to look fear in the face. You are able to say to yourself, 'I lived through this horror, I can take the next thing that comes along . . .' You must do the thing you think you cannot do.'" She learned that "No one can make you feel inferior without your consent."[4]

Eleanor Roosevelt definitely knew that she had to take action even though she felt fear. We need to "know fear," not look for "no fear." So many times we want to dismiss fear and keep it away, but fear cannot stop faith and determination. When fear comes knocking on your door, let faith answer and perhaps someday you will be in the history books.

Elizabeth Fry

Elizabeth Fry (1780–1845) was a Quaker minister and European prison reformer. The mother of ten children, Mrs. Fry was invited to do social work in England's Newgate prison. Unaware of prison conditions, she said she found "half naked women, struggling to-gether . . . with the most boisterous violence . . . I felt as if I were going into a den of wild beasts." Mrs. Fry did nothing sophisti-cated to initiate reform but began reading her Bible to prisoners: "There they sat in respectful silence, every eye fixed upon . . . the gentle lady . . . never till then, and never since then, have I heard anyone read as Elizabeth read."

From such simple beginnings, Fry went on to such innovations as suggesting that men and women be segregated in prison, that more violent offenders be kept from the less violent, and that pris-oners be employed in some useful work. Her influence ranged throughout France and the British Colonies.[5]

I admire the fact that although Elizabeth Fry did nothing so-phisticated to help bring prison reform, she did do what she could do. She read the Bible to the prisoners. Most of the world never does anything about the atrocities that confront society because they feel that what they could do would be so insignificant that it would not matter anyway. Elizabeth disproves that theory. If you will do what you can do, God will do what you cannot do. Doors will open, a way will be made, and creative ideas will come. You will also inspire others to do what they can do and even though each person can only do a little, together we can make a big difference.

Mary McLeod Bethune

Mary McLeod Bethune (1875–1955) was one of the most remark-able black women of her time. A graduate of Moody Bible Insti-tute, she opened a school for black girls in Daytona Beach, Florida. It later became co-educational, and Bethune became in-creasingly involved in government work. From 1935–1944 she was a special advisor on minority affairs to President Franklin Roosevelt. She was the first black woman to head a federal agency and worked to see that blacks were integrated into the military.

She also served as a consultant on interracial affairs at the charter conference of the United Nations. Bethune founded the National Council of Negro Women and was director of Negro Affairs for the National Youth Administration. The fifteenth of seventeen children born to slave parents, she came to have unrestricted access to the White House during Roosevelt's life.[6]

Please note that Mary Bethune was the first woman to head a federal agency. I admire those who are the first to do anything simply because the one who goes first endures more opposition than those who follow later. They are pioneers, and they open the way and pay the price for future generations.

Margaret Thatcher

Margaret Thatcher (born 1925) became Britain's first woman prime minister in 1979 and continued until 1990 when she voluntarily stepped down. She was the first prime minister to be elected three times to office in the twentieth century. Thatcher came up the political ladder with little encouragement. She was the daughter of a grocery owner and Methodist lay preacher and won distinction at Oxford earning degrees in chemistry and law. When she became active in Tory politics, she served as Secretary of State for Education and Science. She expressed her philosophy of leadership this way: "There can be no liberty unless there is economic liberty. . . . Extinguish free enterprise and you extinguish liberty." She also said: "In politics, if you want anything said, ask a man. If you want anything done, ask a woman."[7]

I get irritated with people who are proud of all their knowledge and degrees and yet never do anything remarkable. They especially irritate me when they judge those who are less educated but accomplish great things.

A confident woman may be a deep thinker, but she will also be an activist. She will take action when it is needed. Don't be the kind of woman that thinks something to death. There is a time to think and a time to act, so make sure you know the difference. Margaret Thatcher had a brilliant mind and was highly educated, but she was also a doer.

Mary Fairfax Somerville

Mary Fairfax Somerville (1780–1872) completed all of one year at a woman's boarding school and is considered one of the greatest scientists of her day—but she had to learn her science the hard way. The only daughter of a Scottish admiral, she studied *Elements* by Euclid and an algebra text obtained from her brother's tutor. From this unpromising beginning, she worked her way up to Newton's *Principles* and went on to study botany, astronomy, higher mathematics and physics. Her textbook *Mechanism* became a standard in astronomy and higher mathematics for most of the nineteenth century, and *Physical Geography* caused her to be recognized throughout Europe. She became an honorary member of the Royal Astronomical Society.[8]

Mary proved that there is always a way for the determined woman. She did not give up in the face of difficulties and what seemed to be insurmountable disadvantages. Don't give up your dreams either. Keep pressing forward!

Theodora

Theodora, Empress of Byzantium (502–548) married Justinian, who ruled from 527–565, but it was his wife, a former actress, who saw to it that important legislation was passed and demonstrated the initiative to save her husband's rule by resisting a revolt in 532. Justinian was ready to flee when Theodora persuaded him to defend the capital. In the end he won power for thirty more years, during which time Theodora's name appeared in almost all important laws, including prohibitions against white slavery and the altering of divorce laws to make them more humane to women.

When it came to religion, she strongly supported expressions of the Christian faith upholding the divinity of Christ. After her death in 548, her husband passed practically no important legislation.[9]

> I wonder just how many men have gotten credit for the accomplishments of the great women standing behind them?

They say that behind every great man there is a great woman. I wonder just how many men have gotten credit for the accomplishments of the great women standing behind them? How many great inventors and creators were women forced to turn in their patents and ideas under their husbands' names? History has not been fair to women. If it had been, we would see our history pages filled with accounts of great women who have done remarkable things.

Harriet Beecher Stowe

Harriet Beecher Stowe (1811–1896) wrote what is probably the best-selling American novel of the nineteenth century, a truly Christian work by the title of *Uncle Tom's Cabin*.

A daughter of the famous preacher Lyman Beecher, she took an early interest in theology and works for social improvement. The large Beecher clan moved to Cincinnati where Lyman took over Lane Theological Seminary. There, Harriet Beecher came in contact with fugitive slaves and learned from friends and from personal visits what life was like for a black in the South. When her husband Calvin Stowe was named a professor at Bowdoin College in Maine, she was encouraged to write a book about the evils of slavery by a sister-in-law. The resulting classic sold over 300,000 copies in a year, a sales number absolutely unheard of at the time. The book was later turned into a play by G. L. Aiken and had a long run throughout the country, both before and after the war.[10]

At a time in our country's history when politics and cultural change were still very much a man's world, Harriet made her own mark as one of the most well-known writers of the nineteenth and twentieth centuries. She stood up to misguided and misinformed cultural and racial notions of the day and worked hard to ensure that people everywhere could experience freedom, regardless of their skin color. She was also credited with even bigger things. President Abraham Lincoln, when meeting her in 1862 during the Civil War, reportedly said "So you're the little woman who wrote the book that started this great war!"

Dorothea Lynde Dix

Dorothea Lynde Dix (1802–1887) initiated the most widespread reform for the mentally ill that occurred during the nineteenth century, both in America and in Europe. Her father was an alcoholic preacher and her mother was not in good mental health herself. From early in life she taught school, encouraged by her fiancé Edward Bangs.

Though she decided not to marry him, and in fact remained single throughout her lifetime, Edward continued to encourage her in her teaching and in her social work. Her first experience in mental health reform came about as a result of an opportunity to conduct a Sunday school class in a Cambridge, Massachusetts, jail where she found mentally ill people kept in unheated cells because "the insane do not feel heat or cold." Her reforms first carried the day in Massachusetts, helped along by her friends Bangs and the governor, who knew her personally. From there she traveled throughout the eastern United States, presenting careful research to legislators who usually enacted some kind of reform. One of the conclusions of her research, which had an impact on mental health care both in America and in Europe, was that by merely improving the living conditions of the mentally ill their illness could be greatly alleviated. One source states that Dix played a major role in founding thirty-two mental hospitals, fifteen schools for the feeble minded, a school for the blind, and numerous training facilities for nurses.[11]

All that must happen in order for a tragic injustice to crumble is for someone to confront it. That person must have perseverance and must not be easily defeated by opposition. Dorothea had the qualities that were necessary. It is totally amazing what one woman can accomplish if she will press forward confidently rather than shrinking back in fear and assuming that she could never do the job that needs to be done.

Rosa Parks

Rosa Parks (1913–2005) was the unknown seamstress who started the modern American Civil Rights Movement. On Dec. 1, 1955, she refused to move to the back of the bus after a white man got on board and wanted to sit in a front seat in the city of Montgomery, Alabama. What is not so well known is that this act of defiance to segregationist laws was long planned by a woman well qualified to go into history as initiating the civil rights movement. Born Rosa Louise McCauley in Tuskegee, Rosa was eleven when she attended the Montgomery Industrial School for Girls, a private school founded by women from the northern states. The school supported the philosophy of Rosa's mother who believed "you should take advantage of the opportunities, no matter how few they were."

Rosa also related in later interviews that her lifelong acquaintance with fear made her determined and gave her courage to appeal her conviction during the bus boycott that followed her arrest and conviction. She had already worked on numerous cases with the NAACP before the bus incident. Following Parks' arrest, blacks boycotted the bus system for 382 days until an agreement was worked out. The U.S. Supreme Court also ruled that segregation on buses was unconstitutional. Parks was the first woman to receive the Martin Luther King Nonviolent Peace Prize.[12]

From Rosa's life, we see that if one person is courageous enough to step out and attempt to do something about a problem, other people with the same desire will also come forward. Rosa refused to live in fear; she was determined to have what was rightfully hers and her determination sparked government reform for all.

Judging from some of the testimonies we just read, I would say that women are definitely not "the weaker sex." Their contribution to the world has been magnificent and cannot be ignored any longer.

The Differences between Men and Women—and Weakness Has Nothing to Do with It

God made men and women to be different in many different ways, but muscle mass is just one of those differences. Though men are usually physically stronger than women, this fact certainly does not make women "the weaker sex." It should not apply to our intelligence or our emotions and we should not allow it to!

Whether you are married or single, you will encounter and need to deal with men throughout your life. I believe it is important for our confidence level as women to understand ourselves and the differences between us and men. We need to remember that those differences aren't better or worse, they're just different; once we accept those differences, we can understand and appreciate what each of our genders offer.

Let's start with physical differences. Women's hearts beat faster. Men's brains are larger but women's brains contain more neurons. Depending on whether you're studying the brain of a man or a woman, different areas of the brain will light up in response to identical tasks. Even the rate at which we visibly age is seen differently in men and women.[13]

In his best-selling book, *Love and Respect,* Dr. Emerson Eggerichs points out that the obvious differences found in men and

I don't have to compete with a man for his position, I have my own position and I am comfortable with it.

women can be seen in something as simple as looking into a closet. Eggerichs writes about a couple getting dressed for the day:

> She says, "I have nothing to wear." (She means, she has nothing new.)
> He says, "I have nothing to wear." (He means, he has nothing clean.)[14]

Some women have such a competitive spirit with men that they forget to be women. Recently a minister whom I greatly respect paid me a tremendous compliment. He said, "Joyce, you are a woman in ministry that still knows how to be a woman. You are not trying to act like a man or preach like one." He went on to share that he felt I was strong but feminine and he admired that. He told me that throughout his years in ministry and church leadership he saw many women fail in ministry because they tried to act like men and it caused them to be disliked and rejected.

I am sure we have all heard the saying, "It's a man's world and if you want anything in this world you have to fight for it." I choose to believe it is my world also and I don't fight—I trust God that He will help me be all I can be. I don't have to compete with a man for his position, I have my own position and I am comfortable with it. I like being a woman and I don't want to be a man. But, I must admit there are mornings when I wish all I had to do was comb my hair and shave instead of doing my skin care routine, putting on makeup, curling my hair, arching my eyebrows and trying on three outfits before I finally feel it is safe to go outside.

The Bible says that people are destroyed for a lack of knowledge (Hosea 4:6). I believe marriages, friendships, and business relationships are destroyed due to men and women not understanding the differences that make us unique. In our pride we usually think that we are a shining example of what is right and we expect everyone to act as we do and like what we like, but that is fantasy, not fact.

One man said, "I know I'm not ever going to understand women. I'll never understand how you can take boiling hot wax, pour it onto your upper lip, rip the hair out by the root, and still be afraid of a spider."

Let's look at some other ways men and women are different from each other:

Women offer unsolicited advice and give direction, but men usually don't take advice very well. The woman thinks she is just trying to help, but the man thinks she doesn't trust him to make the right decision.

When a woman disagrees with a man he takes it as disapproval and it ignites his defenses. Men only want advice after they have done everything they can do. Advice given too soon or too often causes him to lose his sense of power. He may become lazy or insecure.

Men are motivated and empowered when they feel needed. Women are motivated when they feel cherished.

Men are visual creatures; once an image is in their head, it's hard to get it out. Women are more inclined to remember emotions or how something made them feel.

Men tend to go into their cave and want to think about what is bothering them, but women want to talk about what's bothering them.

In one survey, more than 80% of men, four out of five, said that in a conflict they were likely to feel disrespected. Women, on the other hand, would feel unloved.[15]

Because a woman's vocal cords are shorter than a man's, she can actually speak with less effort than he can. Shorter vocal cords not only cause a woman's voice to be more high pitched, but also require less air to become agitated, making it possible for her to talk more with less energy expended.[16]

Communication experts say that the average woman speaks more than 25,000 words a day while the average man speaks only a little over 10,000. One business executive said, "The problem is, that by the time I get home from work I have already spoken my 10,000 and my wife hasn't even gotten started."

Men don't feel like they have to share everything while women usually share everything and more. I've seen this occur in my own marriage when I don't feel well and have a virus. Of course, I tell my husband Dave the moment I am not feeling good, and I've been surprised to find while sharing my symptoms in detail that he had the same virus one week earlier and never said one thing to me about it.

When a man and woman have had a problem and the man is ready to reconnect, the woman waits for him to initiate a conversation about what upset him. However, he doesn't need to talk about his upset feelings because he is no longer upset. He wants to forget it and move on, she wants to talk about it and make a list of ways they can avoid having it happen again.

Before I learned better I always wanted to try to figure out why we had the problem or argument to begin with and Dave simply said, "It is part of life."

Men are simple . . . women are not simple and they always assume that men are just as complicated and intricate as they are. The whole point is that guys don't think deeply all the time like women do. They are just what they appear to be.

I recall once getting irritated with Dave and telling him that we needed to have deeper conversation. I shared that I was tired of conversations with no real depth or meaning. He looked very confused and asked me what in the world I was talking about and then went on to say, "This is as deep as I get."

While I have always been a deep thinker and absolutely love to sit and talk and talk and talk about all the possibilities of a situation, Dave keeps it very simple and merely says, "We'll see what happens."

Women want to be loved, respected, valued, complimented, listened to, trusted and sometimes, just to be held. Men want tickets for the World Series.

Women want affection, men want sex.

Most women cry an average of five times per month. I haven't seen my husband cry five times in forty years. Women are simply more emotional than men. Men are very logical.

Understanding does make all the difference in the world. My husband, for example, is very protective of me and is constantly telling me how to do things to prevent me from getting hurt. Before I understood why he gave me instructions on everything from how to get out of the bathtub to how to go down the steps, I thought that he thought I was dumb. I often said, "You don't need to tell me that, I am not stupid." He would look hurt and say "I'm just trying to help you."

Now that I understand, his actions make me feel cherished. The Bible encourages us to seek understanding. Read a couple of good books on the differences between men and women and also one on the differences in personalities. If you do, it will give you insight and understanding that may prevent thousands of arguments or misunderstandings.

Chapter Ten

STEPS TO INDEPENDENCE

Several studies show that women are more likely to be dependent on others than men are and often have more difficulty establishing their independence. This does not mean that women are by nature weaker and more dependent; it means that some of their training has not been as balanced as it should have been.

When girls are growing up they usually spend more time with their mothers than their fathers. A boy begins to realize that he is not like his mother and he differentiates himself from her. His masculinity is defined by separation. This does not mean that he gets away from his mother or no longer needs or depends on her, but it means that he will normally seek his own identity and individuality. A girl does not feel this need and usually remains close to her mother.

Some mothers have great difficulty allowing their sons to find their own identity. They sense them pulling away and it frightens them. If a mother is successful in preventing this healthy separation in her son it can and usually does cause tremendous problems in his life later on.

These facts help form the way we cope with issues when we grow up. Males are often known to be good at independence but not good at relationships. Females are usually better at relationships but not so good with independence.

As much as six times more women experience depression and

about 70% of the mood-altering or anxiety relieving drugs are taken by women.

This reason has been suggested by Maggie Scarf:

> *"Women are statistically more depressed because they have been taught to be more dependent and affection-seeking, and thus they rarely achieve an independent sense of self. A woman gives her highest priorities to pleasing others, being attractive to others, being cared for, and caring for others. Women receive ferocious training in a direction that leads away from thinking "What do I want?" and toward "What do they want?" They may be in danger of merely melting into the people around them and fail to realize they are an individual with rights and needs and they need to establish independence."*[1]

Let me establish what I mean by independence. We are never to be independent from God. As I have said repeatedly, we cannot do anything properly without Him and should be dependent on God at all times for all things.

> *For from Him and through Him and to Him are all things. [For all things originate with Him and come from Him; all things live through Him and all things center in and tend to consummate and to end in Him] To Him be glory forever! Amen (so be it.)* (Romans 11:36)

I have pondered this Scripture for quite some time and I believe it helps make my point. God is everything and we are nothing without Him.

Needing God and needing people is not a sign of weakness. We can be dependent and independent at the same time. Bruce Wilkinson once said that "God's power under us, in us, surging through us, is exactly what turns dependence into unforgettable experiences

It has been statistically proven that 10% of people will never like you so stop trying to have a perfect record with everyone and start celebrating who you are.

of completeness." We can feel complete when we acknowledge our dependence on our Heavenly Father.

I believe that women have a need to feel safe and cared for and I don't believe that is wrong. My husband takes very good care of me and I like it. He is protective and always wants to make sure that I am safe. The difference in me and perhaps someone who has an out of balance attitude in this area is that, even though I thoroughly enjoy Dave taking care of me, I also know that I could take care of myself if I needed to. Even though I am dependent upon him and rightfully so, I am not so dependent that I am handicapped by it.

A balanced independence is what we should seek and to me that is being able to trust and depend on God and other people and yet establish my individual identity. The Bible teaches that we are not to be conformed to the pattern of this world (Romans 12:2). Everyone has their own idea of what we should be. To establish a balanced independence in our lives there are several things we must do.

1. Break Away from Other People's Expectations

Don't let the people around you determine your values or behavior patterns. It seems that everyone expects something a little different, but one thing for sure is that they all expect us to keep them happy and give them what they want.

Many times the expectations people put on us and we accept are unrealistic. If you want to have confidence you must stop trying to be "superwoman." Realize you have limitations and that you cannot keep all the people happy all the time.

It has been statistically proven that 10% of people will never like you so stop trying to have a perfect record with everyone and start celebrating who you are. A person who knows how to live independently does not allow the moods of other people to alter theirs. A story is told of a Quaker man who knew how to live independently as the valued person God had created Him to be. One night as he was walking down the street with a friend he stopped at a news stand to purchase an evening paper. The storekeeper was very sour, rude and unfriendly. The Quaker man treated him with respect and was quite kind in his dealing with him. He paid for his paper and he and his friend continued to walk down the street. The friend said to the Quaker, "How could you be so cordial to him with the terrible way he was treating you?" The Quaker man replied, "Oh, he is always that way; why should I let him determine how I am going to act?"

This is one of the amazing traits we see in Jesus. He was the same all the time. He changed people, they did not change Him.

When an unhappy person is unsuccessful in making you unhappy they begin to respect and admire you. They see that your Christianity is something real and they may be interested in hearing what you have to say.

Even people who seek to control you will disrespect you if you allow them to do it. I encourage you to be your own person. Do what God expects you to do and don't live under the tyranny of other people's expectations.

2. Learn to Cope with Criticism

No matter what you do in life you will be criticized by someone so you must learn to cope with it and not let it bother you. Criticism is very difficult for most of us and a person's self-image can be damaged by one critical remark. But it is possible to learn how not to be affected at all by criticism. Every great man or woman has had to learn how to cope with criticism. Margaret Thatcher once said that if her critics saw her walking along the Thames, they would say it was because she couldn't swim. Actor Dustin Hoffman considered a good review from his critics to simply be a "stay of execution." We must know our own hearts and not allow others to judge us. Like many other great people the Apostle Paul experienced criticism about many things. He experienced the same thing we do, which is that people are fickle. They love you when you are doing everything they want you to do and are quick to criticize when just one little thing goes wrong. Paul said that he was not in the least bit concerned about the judgments of others. He said that he did not even judge himself. He knew he was in God's hands and that in the end he would stand before God and give an account of himself and his life. He would not stand before any man to be judged (1 Corinthians 4:3, 4).

Sometimes the people who are criticized the most are the ones who try to do something constructive with their life. It amazes me how people who do nothing want to criticize those who try to do something. I may not always do everything right, but at least I am attempting to do something to make the world a better place and to help hurting people. I believe that is very pleasing to God! After many years of suffering over the criticisms of people and trying to gain their approval, I finally decided that if God is happy with me, that is enough.

Each time someone criticizes you, try making a positive affirmation about yourself to yourself. Don't just stand by and take in everything anyone wants to dump on you. Establish independence! Have your own attitude about yourself and don't be defeated by criticism. Look at criticism the way Winston Churchill did. During his last year in office, he attended an official ceremony. Several rows behind him two gentlemen began whispering. "That's Winston Churchill." "They say he is getting senile." "They say he should step aside and leave the running of the nation to more dynamic and capable men."

When the ceremony was over, Churchill turned to the men and said, "Gentlemen, they also say he is deaf!"[2]

3. Do Something Outrageous

I think it may be good to occasionally (or perhaps frequently) do something that seems outrageous to people and perhaps even to you. Do something that people won't expect. It will keep your life interesting and keep other people from thinking they have you tucked away nicely in a little box of their own design.

One great woman who was seventy-six years of age said that her goal was to do at least one outrageous thing every week. People become bored because their lives become predictable. A recent Gallup Poll said that 55% of workers "are not engaged" in their workplace.[3] In other words, they show up but have no real interest in being there.

We are not created by God to merely do the same thing over and over until it has no meaning left at all. God is creative. If you don't think so then just look around you. All the animals, bugs, plants, birds, trees and other things are totally amazing. The sun, moon and stars, planets, space, and gravity—all of which God has created—can boggle our minds. We could actually go on forever talking about the infinite variety of things God has created. In case you haven't noticed, God is quite outrageous and frequently changes things up in our lives. He is full of surprises and yet totally dependable. You know, we really can learn a lot from God!

I don't want people to think they have me all figured out and although I want to be dependable and faithful I don't always want to be predictable. Sometimes I get bored with myself and I have to pray and ask God for a creative idea to shake up my life a little and keep me on my toes.

Doing something outrageous means different things to different people. For one it might mean climbing Mount Everest and to another it might mean a clothing style change. I have always liked a certain type of clothing. I liked lots of glitz and everything very fancy. My children kept trying to get me to keep up with changing styles and I firmly resisted for quite a while. They kept saying,

"C'mon Mom, start styling." At first I told them, "I can't dress like that, I am sixty-two." Then God told me to stop making decisions based on my age and I decided I would do something outrageous, something totally unexpected and change my dress-code. My children finally convinced me that just because I was in my sixties I didn't have to dress like it. They wanted me to wear jeans, boots and belts hanging on my hips. One day I made a decision that I was going to shock them so I changed my wardrobe style. I blessed other people with a lot of my fancier clothes and I got a lot of what was in style. I have decided that from now on I am going to dress up to date no matter how old I am.

As a matter of fact, my youngest son Danny was quite delighted when we did a corporate conference with a very popular Christian music group called Delirious, and after much encouragement I finally agreed to wear a nice jeans outfit that night. I actually had the largest altar call that night I've ever had in the United States so my son now reminds me that denim does not hinder the flow of God's power.

Don't get into a rut which is said to be a grave with no ends. Keep life fresh and exciting and try doing some outrageous things. Not stupid things, but outrageously creative and different for you.

4. Have Your Own Opinion

Opinions are very interesting because we all have different ones. You are entitled to your opinion but that does not mean you should always give it to others. Most of the time people don't want our opinions and even if they do ask for it they hope we agree with them. Wisdom knows when to keep quiet and when to talk.

Although we should be wise about how freely we give our opinion we should resist letting popular opinion become ours just because it is popular. Know what you believe and why you believe it!

Our youngest son, Danny, said one day to his father and me in regard to his faith, "I don't know if I believe what I believe because

I believe it or because you believe it." As a child growing up in a Christian home and a ministry family it is easy to sort of be grafted in and not be sure if you are where you are because you want to be or because everyone else wants you to be. I am glad Dave and I recognized that what Danny was going through was not only normal but healthy. I don't want my children to merely have my faith, but I want them to have their own. He went through a period of soul searching, he took some time away by himself and came to a place of knowing what he believed and learning why he believes it.

Parents should not be afraid to let their children explore and discover for themselves what they believe. One of the things people must do to maintain independence is separate from their parents and establish their own identity.

All of our children work with us and that might not sound like much separation but in actuality they are all truly their own person. A healthy separation from parents is not a bad thing, it is good.

Far too many children spend their entire lives in their parents' shadow and that is not a healthy place to be. The actress Marlo Thomas was concerned about being compared to her actor father, Danny Thomas. Could she ever be as funny as him or as good as him? But her dad helped her right from the beginning. He told her she was a thoroughbred, and that thoroughbreds never watched other horses, they simply ran their race. Just before she was to go on stage for her first role in Summer Stock, a package arrived from her father. It was a pair of horse blinders with a note that said, "Run your own race, kid!"

5. Refuse to Pretend

Wanting to please people is not necessarily an abnormal trait but many times we often find that we simply cannot be what they want us to be. However, the mistake that many people make is that they decide to pretend. As one person said to me one day, "I'll

I believe that not being true to one's own self is one of the biggest joy thieves that exist.

just fake it until I make it." That is being untrue to yourself and something you should never do. Jesus did not appreciate the hypocrites, the pretenders and phonies. Even if what you are right now is not what you know you should be, at least be real.

Don't spend your life pretending that you like things you despise, or being with people all the time that you don't enjoy and pretending that you do. I called a pastor one day to ask his advice about letting an employee go. I wanted to do the right thing but after several years of trying I just could not be with this particular person and enjoy her. I don't think there was anything wrong with either of us; we just didn't adapt well to each other. We both had strong personalities and though I was "the boss" and she had to submit to my wishes, I could always feel the war inside her when she didn't like what I was doing, which was most of the time. My pastor friend said something that was very freeing to me. He said, "Joyce, I have finally decided that I am too old and have been doing this too long to spend the rest of my life working with people I don't like and pretending that I do."

To some people this type of thinking might sound very "un-Christian" but it really isn't. Jesus told us to love everyone but He did not say we had to love being with everyone. There are people in life that we simply don't fit with. Our personalities don't blend and work well together. We can call on the power of God and behave ourselves properly when we need to be together, but to try and be together in a close working relationship day in and day out is not a good thing. I made a change and we were both better off for it. She was released to go on to some things she enjoyed much more and I no longer had to pretend to be happy with a situation that I really was not happy with.

Yes, sad to say the world is full of pretenders. People pretend to be happy when they are miserable, they try to do jobs that are way over their head just because they feel they "should" in order to be admired or to maintain a certain reputation with people. People have many masks and can become quite adept at changing them as need be. I believe that not being true to one's own self is one of the biggest joy thieves that exist. Ralph Waldo Emerson pointed out that "to be yourself in a world that is constantly trying to make you something else is the greatest accomplishment." Always remember that to establish independence you must not be a pretender. Be yourself!

6. Say "No!" When You Need To

Anyone who says "yes" to everyone all the time is headed for trouble. When people want you to do something, they definitely won't be happy if you tell them "No," but sooner or later you must decide if you're going to spend your life making other people happy at the expense of never being happy yourself.

There should always be times when we do things for other people just because we want to make them happy, even if the thing they want is not what we would prefer doing. To live that way all the time, however, is not healthy emotionally or in any other way.

Country singer Wynonna Judd knows what can happen when you don't think about yourself. At 17, she had accepted Christ, but the whirlwind years of fame and fortune had created a deep sense of insecurity for her. She felt like she had to take care of everyone. She worked through two pregnancies so she could ensure that the thirty families of her crew would continue to have an income; she ate when she felt empty inside and she spent enormous amounts of money on her family and friends, including the homeless people she sometimes brought into her home.

The need to please everyone eventually caught up with her and in 2004, Wynonna found herself overweight, out of money, guilt-stricken and close to losing her 525-acre farm. She had to surrender to God and start taking care of herself again. She's now twenty pounds lighter, she's cut back her excessive spending and she's learned to say "no." She's turning her life around.[4]

A confident woman can say "no" when she needs to. She can endure people's displeasure and is able to reason that if the disappointed person truly wants a relationship with her they will get over their disappointment and want her to be free to make her own decisions.

Sometimes you have to say "no" to others in order to say "yes" to yourself, otherwise you will end up bitter and resentful feeling that somewhere in the process of trying to keep others happy you lost yourself.

Women in particular want to please people, especially their family, but they need to be very aggressive in standing against getting out of balance in this area. You are valuable and you need to do things that you want to do as well as doing things for others.

When you do feel you need to say no, you don't have to give a reason why. So often people want us to justify our decisions and we really don't need to do that. I try to be led by God's Spirit—or another way of saying it is I try to be led by my heart—and sometimes I don't even fully understand why I don't feel something isn't right for me. But I have learned if I do feel that way I am not going to go against my own conscience in order to have everyone happy with me. I often say, "I just don't have peace about it," or "I don't feel right about it," or even a plain old "I don't want to" is sufficient.

There is nothing wrong with giving a reason if you have one but I think we go overboard in trying to explain ourselves sometimes. If an offended person doesn't want to understand, they are never going to no matter how many reasons you give. Follow your heart and keep your peace. Say "no" when you need to and "yes" when you should.

7. Spend Time with People Who Give You Space to Be Yourself

Some people are always trying to get us to conform to preset patterns, but there are those rare individuals who actually encourage individuality and nonconformity. We must spend time with people who accept and affirm us. One of the many things I have appreciated about my husband over the years is that he gives me space and even encourages me to be me. For example, I am a person who likes to spend time alone. When I get to the point where I know I need a few hours or even a few days to have my space I can simply tell Dave that and he is not insecure about it at all. He does not feel as if I am rejecting him, but he understands that is just the way I am.

I recently counseled a woman who said her husband was driving her crazy because he would never give her even one hour alone. He wanted to be with her constantly and she on the other hand needed space. When she tried to explain that to him, he got offended and took her need as a personal rejection. To nurture healthy relationships we must give people space and freedom.

Dave and I work together, we travel together in our ministry, we see each other more than most average married couples and we enjoy it. But, there are times when we need to get away from each other. Dave plays golf or just goes out for several hours and hits golf balls. He goes to baseball or football games and that gives him his space. There are evenings when I say to Dave, "Why don't you go out and hit some golf balls, I need an evening alone," and he says, "Okay, see you later." A few times each year I try to get away by myself to reflect, read, pray and just be quiet for several days at a time and Dave is always understanding of my need. It is wonderful to be married to someone who is secure enough to encourage you to be who you are, and help you celebrate your uniqueness and individual needs. Nobody wants to be made to feel as if there is something wrong with them because they want to do something a little out of the ordinary.

If you are tired of living on the beaten path that everyone else walks on all the time, then venture into the woods. Some people would be afraid they would get lost, but a confident woman expects to have a new experience that might be outrageously wonderful.

Of course if we want to be encouraged in our own individuality and independence, we must sow the same type of freedom and respect into other people's lives. "Live and let live," should be our motto. There was a time in my life when I was rather narrow-minded and I well remember judging and rejecting one woman in particular who was a rather unique nonconformist. She dressed eclectic long before it became stylish. She was not rebellious against authority, but she was unpredictable and determined to live her own life. She was always doing the unexpected. She was sort of like the wind, you never knew exactly what to expect. That bothered me because in those days I was more of a legalist. Everything had to be one way and that was usually my way.

I look back now and think I probably missed out on a great relationship with someone who could have nurtured freedom in me. But, like many people are, I was fearful of living outside the norm.

I am grateful to God that He has shown me that He wants us to have an exciting life filled with variation and creativity. God created us to be individuals who are able to work together for the common good of all.

Now you [collectively] are Christ's body and [individually] you are members of it, each part severally and distinct [each with his own place and function]. (1 Corinthians 12:27)

Be sure to spend time with people who encourage you in your quest to be an individual. Find friends who give you space to be yourself, space to make mistakes and who respect your boundaries.

8. Watch Children

Jesus said we should become like little children if we expect to enter the kingdom of God. I believe that one of the things He was telling us is to study the freedom that children enjoy. They are unpretentious and straightforward; they laugh a lot, they're forgiving and trusting. Children are definitely confident, at least until the world teaches them to be insecure and fearful. I can remember our son Danny at the age of three walking through the shopping mall with Dave and me and saying to people, "I'm Danny Meyer, don't you want to talk to me?" He was so confident that he was sure everyone wanted to know him better.

Our grandson Austin has always been very bold and confident. I remember him being with us where I was doing a partners conference, and a book signing and photo session with our ministry partners. He was about five years old at the time and because he really wanted to, we let him come on the platform and sing a song he learned at school. The next day I was going to spend some time with our partners, sign their books and have pictures made with them. A large crowd was lining up in the building and our daughter and his mother, Laura, found Austin hiding behind a curtain. When she asked him what he was doing, he said, "I am trying to get some rest from all these people." She said, "Austin, why do you think these people are here?" He said, "Well, to take my picture of course!" Because of his simple, childlike confidence, Austin automatically assumed all the people were there to see him.

Children seem to be able to make a game out of anything. They quickly adjust, don't have a problem letting other children be different than they are and are always exploring something new. They are amazed by everything!

Oswald Chambers wrote in *My Utmost for His Highest:* "The freedom after sanctification is the freedom of a child, the things that used to keep the life pinned down are gone." We definitely need to watch and study children and obey the command of Jesus to be more like them (Matthew 18:3). It is something we have to do on purpose as we get older. We all have to grow up and be responsible, but we don't have to stop enjoying ourselves and life.

Don't let the world steal your confidence. Remember that you have been created on purpose by the hand of God. He has a special, unique, wonderful plan for you. Go for it! Don't shrink back, conform, or live in fear.

9. Fight Off Stagnation

Have you ever seen a puddle of water that was stagnant? There's no circulation, no fresh water source, and the water just sits there. If left over time and the sun doesn't evaporate it first, bacteria can form and the water can turn green. There's little life left.

We can slide into stagnation. It happens a little bit at a time and often so slowly that it is almost imperceptible. Once life was exciting and then it seems that suddenly we find ourselves with what the world calls "mid-life crisis." I think it is no more or less than stagnation. We stop being daring, doing outrageous things, and being creative. We settle in, we slip into the world's mold, and we conform to what people expect. We become boringly predictable!

I believe everyone will stagnate if they don't fight it. It is easy to just float along with everyone else doing the same thing every day. Only rare individuals are willing to swim upstream when it would be so easy to float downstream with everyone else. One of the most valuable things I have learned is that there are many things I must do "on purpose." I can't wait to feel like doing them.

For example, I purposely take care of my responsibilities in life, because I know it is very important. I give on purpose. I actually look for people to be a blessing to because I have learned the vitally important lesson that Jesus taught about walking in love (Ephesians 5:2, 2 John 1:6). I purposely do something that is a little out of the ordinary for me every once in a while simply because I refuse to live in stagnation. I purposely spend time every day in prayer and fellowship with God because I want to honor Him and always give Him His rightful place in my life, which is first place.

I wear different pajamas almost every night. Some people could wear the same thing to sleep every night and never get tired of it, but the same pajamas night after night bores me. Whatever it takes for you to keep your life interesting, do it on purpose. If you take this aggressive action, it will make a big difference in the quality of life you have. Don't just put in your time here on earth, enjoy your life and make the world glad that you are here.

10. With God, All Things Are Possible

We began this chapter discussing the need to maintain our individuality. You may remember that I said our goal should be to seek a balanced independence. I believe that balance is the key to success in everything. The Bible states that unless we are well balanced the devil will be able to devour us (1 Peter 5:8). Where there is no balance we always find destruction. A gymnast will never successfully complete a routine unless she can achieve balance in her stance. A scientist will have difficulty completing his experiment if he never learns how to balance his scientific instrument. People who never learn how to balance their checkbook can end up in serious financial trouble. Balance is very important!

God has created us as individuals who need each other. We work the best when we work together. Combining gifts and talents gives us the best result. So we should depend first and foremost on God and then on people, but our dependence on people must remain balanced.

The Bible says that Jesus did not trust Himself to His disciples because He knew the nature of all men (John 2:24). That simply means that although He was in relationship with them, shared His life with them and was dependent on them for certain things, He never allowed that dependence to be such that He could be devastated if they disappointed Him. He knew the nature of people was to be just what they are—people! People made up of flaws and imperfections.

Once I found myself worried about what I would do if Dave died. How could I run the ministry on my own? After several days of this mental attack the Lord spoke to my heart and said, "If Dave died you would keep doing exactly what you are doing, because I am the One holding you up, not Dave." I obviously needed Dave and was dependent on him for many things, but God wanted to establish in my heart from the beginning of our ministry that with or without Dave or anyone else for that matter, I could do what God had asked me do as long as I had Him. Every individual needs to believe this same thing. God is all you have to have. Many other things are nice and comforting, but God is the only person we can never do without. The Bible says that Joseph's brothers hated him, but God gave him favor everywhere he went (Genesis 39:21). It just doesn't matter who is against you as long as God is for you.

When Peter, Judas and others disappointed Jesus, He was not devastated because His confidence was not misplaced. He was dependent and yet independent at the same time. I depend on many people in my ministry to help me accomplish what I am called to do. However, we see constant change. People leave that we thought would be with us forever and God sends new ones that have amazing gifts. We quickly learned that if we don't become overly confident in any one person then we can avoid a lot of worry and concern. We look to God to meet our needs, not people. We need people, but we know it is God working through people to help us. If He decides to change who He works through that should be no concern of ours.

When Mother Teresa left for India to begin her mission work there she was told she could not do it because she had no money and no one to help her. I was told she said she had three pennies and God, and that was all she needed.

All of us are familiar with the amazing work she did to help the poor in India. Her willingness to stand with God alone, having all her confidence in Him allowed God to work through her in a remarkable way.

She was a rare individual who knew how to work with people, but who believed that with or without people she could do all God was asking her to do.

That is the kind of attitude I want to maintain. I appreciate all the wonderful people God has placed in my life. My husband and children are amazing. Our ministry staff is top notch and the wonderful ministry partners God has given us are awesome. I need all of them but if for any reason God ever decided to remove any of them from my life I want to be a confident woman who knows that with God alone all things are possible. My confidence must be in Him more than it is in anything or anyone else.

PART
II

Living Boldly and Without Fear

Chapter Eleven

THE ANATOMY OF FEAR

Fear. We've all experienced it. It's that unsettled feeling you get in your stomach, it's the panic that can overtake you with no notice. Everyone is inevitably afraid of something. After all, we're human. In fact, according to a recent study, 19.2 million American adults age 18 and over, or about 8.7% of people in this age group in a given year, are scared of something specific. Fifteen million Americans have social phobias that make it difficult to interact with other people due to being extremely self-conscious in social situations.[1]

A popular television show actually challenges contestants to face their fears to the extreme—lying down in aquariums filled with crabs or snakes, jumping out of helicopters or eating live spiders or other insects. It's not my idea of a fun time, but most of the people who participate probably aren't doing it for fun either; they're trying to win the $50,000 awarded at the end of the show. Eventually someone is challenged with a stunt that is too scary. Unable to overcome their fear, the player gives up and walks away.

Life often brings fear into the picture and many times we can feel like that contestant—ready to give up and walk away. If we ever want to overcome uncertainty and doubt, if we ever truly want to become confident women, it's vital that we have a complete and thorough understanding of the nature and anatomy of fear. The first thing we must know is that fear does not come from God. He has not given us a spirit of fear (2 Timothy 1:7).

Fear torments and prevents progress. It causes people who should be bold and aggressive to shrink back, to hide and be cowardly and timid. Fear is a thief. It steals our destinies. As I said in

If we ever want to overcome uncertainty and doubt, if we ever truly want to become confident women, it's vital that we have a complete and thorough understanding of the nature and anatomy of fear.

an earlier chapter, the only acceptable attitude we should have toward fear is "I WILL NOT FEAR!" Each of us must be firm in our resolve that we will not allow fear to rule in our lives. There is far too much at stake to take a light attitude toward this huge problem.

I believe that fear is the master spirit that the devil uses against people. Think about the problems you currently have. How many of those are tied to fear? I bet if you think about it, you will say most have something to do with being afraid. Our worries come from fear. We try to control people and circumstances due to fear. We let people control us because of fear. People who are afraid of being poor become greedy and stingy. Someone who is afraid of not having friends pretends to be someone they're not. We get into wrong and harmful relationships due to the fear of being lonely, and the list goes on and on. However, I believe we can conquer fear if we make time to understand it and see fear for what it really is, a spirit that has no place in a life turned over to Christ.

I once heard a story of a village where the children were told by their parents: "Whatever you do, don't go near the top of the mountain. It's where the monster lives." All the previous generations of children heeded this warning and avoided going near the top of the mountain.

One day, some brave young men in the village decided that they had to go and see the monster. They wanted to see what it was really like and defeat it. So they loaded their packs with provisions and set off up the mountain. Halfway up, they were stopped in their tracks by a huge roar and a terrible stench. Half the men ran down the mountain, screaming.

The other half of the group continued on their journey. As they got farther up the mountain, they noticed that the monster was smaller than they had expected—but it continued to roar and emit such a stench that all but one of the men ran back down the mountain into the village.

"I am going to get the monster," the one remaining man said to himself, and he took another step forward. As he did so, the monster shrank until it was the same size as the man. As he took another step toward the monster, it shrank again. It was still hideously ugly and continued to emit the stench, but the man was so close to the monster now that he could actually pick it up and hold it in the palm of his hand. As he looked at it, he said to the monster, "Well, then, who are you?"

In a tiny, high-pitched voice, the monster squeaked: "My name is Fear."[2]

This story gives such an accurate description of the way fear works. It seems so monstrous and horrible until you begin to confront it, but the more you confront it, the smaller it becomes. If you follow God's plan for conquering fear, you will find one day that the things which frightened you the most were really nothing at all. What once roared at you will only squeak and eventually become totally silent.

Always remember what Franklin Roosevelt once pointed out: the one thing we must fear is fear itself; for indeed if we allow it to, it will control us. If we confront it, we will master it.

Fears and Phobias

Fears can develop from almost anything. Here's a short list of some of the more bizarre fears people experience.

Peladophobia: fear of baldness and bald people.

Aerophobia: fear of drafts.

Porphyrophobia: fear of the color purple.

Chaetophobia: fear of hairy people.

Levophobia: fear of objects on the left side of the body.

Dextrophobia: fear of objects on the right side of the body.

Auroraphobia: fear of the northern lights.

Calyprophobia: fear of obscure meanings.

Thalassophobia: fear of being seated.

Stabisbasiphobia: fear of standing and walking.

Odontophobia: fear of teeth.

Graphophobia: fear of writing in public.

Phobophobia: fear of being afraid.

(From *Nothing to Fear*, by Fraser Kent, Doubleday & Company, 1977)

The variety of phobias that people suffer with are seemingly endless and some of them quite bizarre, but they are very real and stifling to the one who suffers. Some people have fears so unique that they are afraid to share their fears. The best way to overcome anything is to expose it. Anything hidden has power over us, but once it is brought into the light it can be dealt with and overcome.

Don't Shrink from Confrontation

In April 2005, many Americans and the world heard the story of the "runaway bride," Jennifer Wilbanks. The thirty-two-year-old Duluth, Georgia, resident disappeared just days before her 600-guest wedding was to take place. Her family and fiancé, certain she had been kidnapped, pleaded for her safe return and the missing bride became a national story for the major news media.

When she turned up alive and okay on the other side of the country, joy that she'd been found quickly turned into confusion and anger as the truth revealed that Wilbanks hadn't been kidnapped but left because of wedding day jitters. An Associated

Press story reported that the bride-to-be ran because of "certain fears" that controlled her life.[3]

Most of us would probably say "well, she should have talked to her fiancé instead of running away." Or at the very least, she should have sought counsel from her pastor or a family member. But how many of us easily confront our fears? Isn't it easier just to ignore something and not deal with it? You may not have ever physically run away like Wilbanks, but I bet emotionally there are things you're running from. You're constantly looking over your shoulder trying to keep whatever you're afraid of from catching up with you.

Confrontation is extremely difficult for many people, but it must be done unless we want other people and other things to control our lives. Did you ever play freeze tag when you were a kid? Whoever you were running from ultimately had control over you because if they ever tagged you, you were instantly frozen, stopped in your tracks. That's the way fear works. What we run from or hide from has power over us.

As I said previously, it's also important to remember that what we hide in the darkness has to be brought into the light if we're going to get rid of it. Go into a completely dark room and switch on the light. What happens? The darkness is swallowed up. That is the way God and His Word work in our lives. When we do what God's Word tells us to do, those fears that try to torment us are swallowed up. They're gone and they have no power over you.

God's Word is pretty clear on this point: we are not to fear. Isaiah 41:10 says "Fear not [there is nothing to fear], for I am with you; do not look around you in terror and be dismayed, for I am your God." Notice that He doesn't say that we are never to feel fear, but He does say we shouldn't allow fear to control us and steal our destiny.

The Fear monster acts much bigger and tougher than it actually is. That's because fear depends on being able to deceive people.

Once a person realizes they can "feel the fear and do it anyway," they are free.

Satan loves causing people to dread and avoid confronting unpleasant issues because he knows that he loses power when his lies are confronted. Think about all of those generations of people in the story I just told who lived their entire lives afraid of something that was actually small enough to be held in one hand. Until someone was brave enough to confront it, someone who refused to run, that little runt of a monster held people tight, leaving them essentially frozen. Even though a lie is not true, it becomes reality for the person who believes it. Don't believe the lies Satan tries to deceive you with.

How I wish I had a magic wand I could wave or a prayer I could say that would end fear in your life once and for all. Unfortunately, that's not going to happen. Prayer does give us the strength to stand against fear, but for us to overcome and be conquerors like God intends us to be, we must have something to overcome and conquer! You would never expect to run three miles without first learning to run one. It's the same way with prayer. God wants us to stretch our faith muscles and stand against fear. He wants us to say "No! Fear is not going to rule in my life." As we learn to use prayer to confront and combat the small fears, He'll help us learn to tackle the bigger fears too.

Don't let fear freeze you into paralysis. Hannah Hurnard, author of *Hinds' Feet on High Places,* was once paralyzed by fear. Then she heard a sermon on scarecrows that challenged her to turn her fear into faith.

The preacher said, "A wise bird knows that a scarecrow is simply an advertisement. It announces that some very juicy and delicious fruit is to be had for the picking. There are scarecrows in all the best gardens . . . If I am wise, I too shall treat the scarecrow as though it were an invitation. Every giant in the way which makes me feel like a grasshopper is only a scarecrow beckoning me to

God's richest blessings." He concluded, "Faith is a bird which loves to perch on scarecrows. All our fears are groundless."[4]

When we do our part, praying and stretching our spiritual muscles as we take these steps of faith, God always does His part, making seemingly impossible things possible.

Partners with God

Have you ever gotten together with a friend to make dinner for your families, or maybe for another family who could use the meal? Maybe she was responsible for the main dish and you fixed the sides. However you assigned the work, each of you had a specific part and together, you completed what needed to be done.

When it comes to life, we need to remember that God is our partner and realize that He has a part and we have a part. When we do our part, praying and stretching our spiritual muscles as we take these steps of faith, God always does His part, making seemingly impossible things possible. Maybe you've had so much fear in your life for so long that right now, you can't see how you can ever be free from it. I promise you—each time you confront fear, it becomes smaller and smaller. Eventually, it will completely lose its power over you.

I hate fear and what it does to people. It makes us withdraw; it makes us retreat. It eats away at our confidence and our self-assurance until all that's left is a skeleton of what there was. But it doesn't have to be that way! I have experienced a lot of fear in my own life and I know it takes a lot of courage to face what you fear the most. But, if I can do it so can you! A wise man once said "Courage is not the lack of fear but the ability to face it." God's promises are not for a specially selected few people, they are for everyone. If God can help anyone at all, then He can help you and He can help you face your fears. God's promises offer hope and an opportunity for a new life for you. A life lived boldly and aggressively instead of by fear and uncertainty.

One of the most confident women we find in the Bible is Esther and her story of rescuing her people from certain death at the hands of an evil and hateful man. Though her beauty didn't hurt, it was her character and quiet confidence that helped her find favor with the king, Xerxes. She took great risk when she made her way to Xerxes' inner court uninvited. But God honored her and the prayers that the other Jews were praying, and Xerxes received her warmly. In the end, Esther saved her people from perishing.

Confidence is holding on to a strong faith in God, a faith that is backed up with a complete knowledge and understanding that with God's help you can do anything. Fear brings a lack of confidence in God and in you. It is a destructive, debilitating belief that you can't. As a woman, you can do amazing things, but you will have to become confident. Replace your fears with confidence and watch what God can do!

I don't think anyone enjoys confrontation or looks forward to it. It is certainly not my favorite thing to do. Most of us don't like to rock the boat and make waves, but I can assure you that taking the steps of whatever you need to do in order to enjoy a life of freedom is definitely not as difficult as staying in bondage for the rest of your life. You have to care enough about yourself and your loved ones to confront fear and start being the person you have always wanted to be. Do it, even if you have to "do it afraid."

Do It Afraid

I have told this story in other books I have written but it bears repeating in this one. There was a woman we will call Joy who literally lived her entire life as far as she could remember in fear. It controlled her. She would not drive a car. She would not go out at night. She was afraid of meeting new people. She was afraid of crowds, new things, airplanes, failure and just about anything else one could imagine. Her name was Joy but she certainly never experienced any because her fears entrapped and tormented her. She so desperately wanted to be brave and courageous. She wanted to have an exciting life and be adventurous but her dreams were constantly squelched by her fears.

Joy was a Christian and one day was lamenting her woes once again to her longtime Christian friend Debbie. Debbie had heard it all many times but this time she responded in a way that shocked Joy. Debbie looked her friend right in the eyes and said forcefully, "Well, why don't you just do it afraid." What a powerful truth! This was the beginning of a new life for Joy because for the first time she saw fear for what it was. Fear was never going to just evaporate from her life. It had been a stronghold for too long and its roots were too deep. Joy had to confront it by simply moving ahead and doing what she wanted to do even if she did it feeling afraid.

Fear means to run away from or to take flight, but confrontation means to face something head-on. Sometimes those confrontations require us to face ourselves—maybe we're fearful of failure or fearful of success. Sometimes the fears or concerns you have will require confronting someone else; maybe a parent or a husband, even a child.

David Augsburger, in his book, *Caring Enough to Confront,* suggests ways you can word things that express your thoughts while at the same time showing that you care about the other person.[5]

Confronting	Caring
I feel deeply about the issue at stake.	I care about our relationship.
I want to clearly express my view.	I want to hear your view.
I want respect for my view.	I want to respect your insights.
I want you to trust me with your honest feelings.	I trust you to be able to handle my honest feelings.
I want you to keep working with me until we've reached a new understanding.	I promise to stay with the discussion until we've reached an understanding.
I want your unpressured, clear, honest view of our differences.	I will not trick, pressure, manipulate, or distort the differences between us.
I want your caring-confronting response.	I give you my loving, honest respect.

Look It in the Eye

Two explorers were on a jungle safari when suddenly a ferocious lion jumped in front of them. "Keep calm," the first explorer whispered. "Remember what we read in that book on wild animals? If you stand perfectly still and look the lion in the eye, he will turn and run." "Sure," replied his companion. "You've read the book, and I've read the book. But has the lion read the book?"

When we decide whether or not to face a situation or to run from it there are many things that go through our mind; we think that there is less risk of us being hurt or someone else being hurt or maybe we simply don't want to take the time to deal with something. Just remember, though, if you run you will have to keep running.

When Adam and Eve sinned in the Garden of Eden the first thing they did was run away and try to hide from the Presence of God. They tried to cover up their nakedness with fig leaves. It didn't work for them and it won't work for us either. God had to intervene with a plan for their redemption and He has one for us.

Take a look at Ephesians 6 in God's Word to His people and notice what battle armor He provides us with. He tells us to stand firm with a belt of truth, a breastplate of righteousness,

> God never intended us to run from our enemies. His plan was and still is that with Him at our side we confront any issue in our life that is a problem.

shoes of the gospel of peace, a shield of faith, a helmet of salvation and the sword of the Spirit. Notice anything missing? There's nothing provided to protect our backside! That's because God never intended us to run from our enemies. His plan was and still is that with Him at our side we confront any issue in our life that is a problem. People are so skilled at not facing real issues and they're even better at trying to cover them up by living make-believe lives and inventing false personalities. It is time to take a stand and confront fear!

A woman attended one of my conferences and testified that it was the first time she had gone out of her home in thirty-five years. As we interviewed her and got more of her story we were even more amazed. As a child, she was abused, and although she did get married and have children of her own she decided that life would be safer for her if she stayed inside where no one could hurt her. She managed different ways of getting the things she needed and with the invention of computers it became much easier for her to be a recluse. She ordered over the Internet and communicated by mail and telephone.[6]

Eventually, she started watching my daily television program and discovered from my testimony that I had also been sexually abused by my father. She decided if I could get up in front of thousands of people and speak boldly that the least she could do was go out of her house. She made the decision to come to my conference and she did, and though she was shaky and very nervous, she was there. That was the first step for her in confronting her fear. She did something afraid. She had a long way to go, but no one can drive a parked car. She had to take one step before she could take two. I hope her story encourages you and motivates you to begin your own journey of breaking free from fear and start moving toward becoming the confident woman that you want to be.

Life changed greatly for me when I finally understood that to fear meant to run from or take flight. I now understand that even if I am shaking as a result of fear that I am not behaving cowardly as long as I keep pressing forward to do whatever it is the fear is trying to get me not to do.

The way to develop confidence is to do the thing you fear, and get a record of successful experiences behind you. Henry Ford said, "One of the greatest discoveries a man makes, one of his great surprises, is to find he can do what he was afraid he couldn't do."[7]

Dave and I recently saw a humorous but informative example of how fear makes one want to run and hide. We have a seven-pound dog who is a Maltese, and she is very white and fluffy. Her name is Duchess, and of course she is just as cute as she can be. Duchess has never liked getting a bath and since she was a puppy, whenever she realizes she is about to get bathed, she starts to shake and runs off to another part of the house and hides. As she got older, she seemed to get over it and was less fearful about it.

But then one summer we were staying at a condo someone let us use and when Duchess heard the word bath and saw me getting out her shampoo and other supplies that I normally use for it, she disappeared. When I finally found her, she was shaking and hiding in another room. At first I didn't know what was wrong with her because she hadn't acted afraid of baths for a while. But then I realized it was the bath and she was afraid because she was in a new situation and a new place.

Even animals respond to fear by running and hiding. They live by instinct and will always respond to those instincts, but thank God we live by making wise choices according to our knowledge of God's Word. His Word says not to give into fear and with help from His Spirit, we can make the right choice.

Is Anyone Immune to Fear?

Are some people cursed to be afraid while others are blessed with being brave? We recognize that we are born with different temperaments. We don't choose them; God chooses them to help us fulfill our purpose in life. Some people are just naturally more aggressive, brave and daring than others but I personally don't believe anyone is totally immune from fear. Even the person you know who appears to be the bravest of all has fear about something.

Some people do a better job than others of hiding their fears. They may not even admit to themselves that they have fears but the reality is that Satan attacks everyone with fear. We can overcome it! If it weren't possible to overcome fear then God would not have instructed us in His Word to "fear not!"

I believe we are all brave in some areas and fearful in others. The pendulum may swing one way or the other, but we all have some of both. For example, a woman we will call Theresa was timid and shy. She didn't talk a lot and was introverted. She would be petrified to stand in front of a crowd of people and speak, and yet Theresa was very brave when it came to facing pain and tragedy in her own life. She had cancer at the age of 32 and endured surgery and painful radiation and chemotherapy treatments. Theresa also had three miscarriages before she finally gave birth to a healthy child. She bore these difficulties graciously, bravely and with little complaint.

Janice, a friend of Theresa's, was very outwardly aggressive. Janice was so outgoing she could have made friends with a telephone pole. She was a leader, spoke easily in front of large groups and was generally admired by all. On the surface Janice did not appear to be fearful at all. Like Theresa, Janice also faced tragedy in her life. For twenty years, she worked for a corporation and had built up a large retirement through investing in a 401(k) matching funds retirement program. Quite to everyone's surprise the company was investigated for fraud concerning the investment of the employees' retirement fund and suddenly Janice as well as many other employees discovered they had no retirement. The company filed bankruptcy and several of the officers were tried and sentenced to prison terms. Not only did Janice suddenly have no retirement, she also had no job. She did not handle her tragedy graciously. She displayed fear that amazed those who knew her. She had always appeared to be so fearless, but in this situation she was almost paralyzed with fear about her future and financial security.

I am bold enough to stand in front of a million people and speak for hours. I have no fear of being transparent and sharing details of my life that many people would not be comfortable sharing. On the other hand, if I got onto a roller coaster at an amusement park I would be shaking and possibly screaming, but not with delight.

During our travels, my husband Dave will try all kinds of food he has never eaten or even seen but I am always looking for something I am familiar with. I am afraid if I try something new that I won't like it and my meal will be ruined. My point is that nobody is really immune from all fear. Some people's fears are more obvious than others, but I believe we all have them.

It's important for us to realize that we are not alone in our battles with fear. The devil wants nothing better than to convince you that there is something really wrong with you or I and that other normal people don't have the same kinds of problems. Don't let him do it; all of us experience fear.

General George Patton would certainly be considered a very brave man and yet he admitted that he had fears. He just chose not to pay attention to them.

During World War II, a military governor met with General George Patton in Sicily. When he praised Patton highly for his courage and bravery, the general replied, "Sir, I am not a brave man . . . The truth is, I am an utter craven coward. I have never been within the sound of gunshot or in sight of battle in my whole life that I wasn't so scared that I had sweat in the palms of my hands." Years later, when Patton's autobiography was published, it contained this significant statement by the general. "I learned very early in my life never to take counsel of my fears."

The spirit of fear is not exclusive for who it visits or when it visits them. Sometimes fear shows up at very inconvenient times, moments when we would prefer to feel fearless. After all, who wants to confront and deal with fear? Nobody does and most people don't! It just seems easier to run or hide or procrastinate. We wish it would go away, we pray it will go away, but until we confront it, fear will always have us on the run. If we are going to run, it needs to be toward the enemy, not away from him.

Variety! Variety! Variety!

The variety of fears that the devil presents to people is endless and amazing. Various people are afraid of everything from dirt to death. I'll mention several that I have either dealt with in trying to help people or have heard of. Fear of being lonely, rejected, abandoned, taken advantage of, intimacy, childbirth, heights, water, bees, dogs, cats, other animals or rodents. Some people are afraid of sickness and they always imagine some new disease is developing in their body. The fear of man is huge and so is the fear of lack. The fear of failure torments many people, while others are afraid of success. Women especially often have a fear of their husbands dying and being left with nothing, something some call the "bag lady syndrome." Some people are almost paranoid about their appearance. Other people have a fear of drowning, germs, elevators, crowds, flying or fire. I know a grown woman who has never struck a match because she is afraid of them. Some people can't form meaningful relationships due to a fear of intimacy.

I could go on but I think you see my point. You may even be a person who experiences a fear that seems so weird you would

What Are We Afraid Of?

A Gallup Poll conducted in 2005 revealed the most common fears of teenagers in the United States. They included:

1. Terrorist attacks
2. Spiders
3. Death
4. Failure
5. War
6. Heights
7. Crime/Violence
8. Being alone
9. The future
10. Nuclear war

never even tell anyone about it. Believe me, someone out there has a fear even stranger than yours. But why do some people have one fear while others have another? Someone who grows up in Florida may be more fearful of hurricanes than someone who grows up in Kansas or Tennessee who has an intense fear of tornadoes. Someone who lives in the city may be more fearful of muggings than someone who lives on a farm. Why can one person be terrified of dogs and someone else love them?

We do know some of the answers but certainly not all of them. I don't think we need to figure out fear nearly as much as we simply need to make up our minds that it is no longer going to control us. Some people spend their entire life trying to figure out their problems and never get around to getting past them. But God can help us get past those fears that attempt to freeze us up, if we'll only look to Him for His help.

Face your fears today and ask God for His help in moving past them. It is only by His grace that we can all overcome our fears!

Chapter Twelve

FEAR HAS RELATIVES

Once you allow the spirit of fear to take hold of your life, you open the door to other spirits that want to grip your heart and cause you to freeze up, unable to move forward in confidence and assurance. Worry and dread are both relatives of the spirit of fear. Or, look at it this way: Fear is the parent and worry and dread are the children. The Bible clearly teaches that God's children are not to worry. When we worry, we rotate our minds around and around a problem and come up with no answers. The more we do it, the more anxious we feel. When we worry, we actually torment ourselves with a type of thinking that produces no good fruit. Worry starts with our thoughts but it affects our moods and even our physical bodies.

Keep in mind that worry doesn't wait until we grow up, either. A study out of the United Kingdom showed that more than half of teenage girls worry about their appearance, one in three are stressed out by school and nearly 40% worry about their families. It's no wonder that 80% of chronic worriers also have a poor self-image—their confidence has been eaten up by fear and doubt disguised as worry![1]

A person can worry so much that it makes them feel depressed and sad. Worry places stress on your entire system and causes a lot of physical ailments like headaches, tension in muscles, stomach problems and many other things. The only thing worry does not do is something good. It never helps and it does not solve our problems.

Jesus said that we should not worry about tomorrow for each

Prayer opens the door for God to get involved and meet our needs.

day has sufficient troubles of its own (Matthew 6:34)! Trying to solve tomorrow's problems today only steals the energy God has prearranged for you in order to enjoy today. Don't waste your time worrying! It is vain and useless. Don't be like the bassoon player who went up to his conductor, and nervously said that he could not reach the high E flat. His conductor just smiled and replied, "Don't worry. There is no E flat in your music tonight." Many of our worries are like that—unfounded and unnecessary.

Humble yourself under God's mighty hand by casting all your care on Him (1 Peter 5:6, 7). In this way you are saying to God, "I know I cannot solve my own problems and I am totally trusting in you to take care of me and give me the answers I need in my situation."

You can only be a confident woman once you remove fear and worry from your life and it starts with prayer. Prayer opens the door for God to get involved and meet our needs. The Apostle Paul said we are to be anxious for nothing, but in all things by praying we will experience the peace of God (Philippians 4:6, 7). He didn't say in "some" things, he didn't say in "one" thing, he said in everything. Prayer must replace our worry.

We can worry about hundreds of different things. From what people think of us to what will happen to us as we age. How long will we be able to work? Who will take care of us when we get old if we are not able to care for ourselves? What happens if the stock market crashes? What if gas prices go up? What if I lose my job? Quite often, worry does not even have a basis or a nugget of truth to it. There is no known reason to even think about the things that worry and then frighten us. Worry can even become a bad habit. It is just what we do! Some people fret over something all the time. If they don't have problems of their own they worry about other people and their problems.

The only answer is to "stop worrying and place your trust in

God." He has the future all planned and He knows the answer to everything. His Word promises us that He will take care of us if we trust in Him.

Someone once said that "Worry is interest paid on trouble before it falls due." Worry believes it will have trouble before it does. It constantly drains the energy God gives us to face daily problems and to fulfill our many responsibilities. It is therefore a sinful waste. Worry is the end of faith and faith is the end of worry.

Don't worry that you might have a rotten day, because if you do have one you will certainly know it and you can deal with it then. You know you're having a rotten day when . . .

Your birthday cake collapses from the weight of the candles.
Your twin sister forgot your birthday.
You call Suicide Prevention and they put you on hold.
Your car horn goes off accidentally and remains stuck as you follow a group of Hells Angels on the freeway.
Your boss tells you not to bother to take off your coat.
The bird singing outside your window is a buzzard.
You wake up and your braces are locked together.
You put both contact lenses in the same eye.
Your husband says, "Good morning, Judy," and your name is Sally.

When Jesus instructed us not to worry about tomorrow, He was saying that we should deal with life one day at a time. He gives us the strength we need as we need it. When we take that strength He gives us and apply it to worry instead of action, we rob ourselves of the blessings God intended for us to have today—not tomorrow or the next, but today. We miss out on good things because we worry about bad things that may not even come to be!

For several years a woman had trouble getting to sleep at night because she feared burglars. One night her husband heard a noise in the house, so he went downstairs to investigate. When he got there, he did find a burglar. "Good evening," said the man of the house. "I am pleased to see you. Come upstairs and meet my wife. She has been waiting ten years to meet you."

Life has its bumps and potholes in the road. You will have enough things to deal with just because you're alive and on planet Earth. Why would anyone want to worry about tomorrow's problems? What we worry about frequently never happens anyway and if it is going to happen, worrying won't prevent it. Worry does not make you escape your trouble, it only makes you unfit to deal with it when it comes.

God is our help in trouble (Psalm 46:1). With worry, you are on your own. When you worry, which do you worry about, what might happen or what might not happen? For worriers, the Scots have a proverb: "What may be, may not be."

A confident woman does not worry because she sees the future differently than women who are worriers. She confidently believes that with God's help she can do whatever she needs to do no matter what it is. Her positive attitude enables her to expect good things in the future, not bad ones. Confidence is the fruit of trusting God. When we trust Him we may not have all the answers, but we are confident that He does.

Don't Worry about Past Mistakes

It is useless to worry about anything and doubly useless to worry about something that is over and done with and that nothing can be done about. If you made a mistake in the past that can be rectified then go ahead and take action to correct it. But, if you cannot do anything about it except be sorry, then ask for forgiveness from God and anyone you may have hurt and don't worry about it any longer.

Let me remind you that worry is useless . . . so why do it? God has given us wisdom and a wise person will not spend their time doing something that produces nothing of any value.

There are many wonderful scriptures in the Bible that teach us to let go of the past and look to the future. We're reminded to forget what is behind and keep our eyes facing forward, on God and His plan for us (Philippians 3:13). We can find peace in the knowledge that God's compassion and kindness is new every morning and that His faithfulness is abundant (Lamentations 3:22, 23). Also, we must never forget that He is able to overcome and do far more than we could ever imagine that He could do for us (Ephesians 3:17, 21). God has provided a way for your past to have zero power over you, but it is up to you to receive His gracious gift of forgiveness, mercy and a new beginning.

Don't allow mistakes in your past to fester and threaten your future. When you ask God to forgive you for something that you have done wrong He is faithful and just to do it. He continuously cleanses us from all unrighteousness (1 John 1:9). It's forgiven and forgotten—but you must do the same!

Get Over Guilt

Millions of people destroy their lives by feeling guilty about something that is in the past and that they cannot do anything about. When God forgives our sin He also removes the guilt. But just as we must receive His forgiveness, we must also receive freedom from guilt and not let the emotion of guilt control us. If God says we are forgiven and pronounced not guilty then we should believe His Word more than how we feel.

We frequently hear people say, "I will feel guilty about that the rest of my life." Or, I have heard people say, "I will never get over what I have done." God's Word says that when He forgives us He forgets the offense and there is no more penalty for sin where there is complete remission of it (Hebrews 10:17, 18). Why decide that you will feel guilty the rest of your life when God has provided a way for you to live free from it?

I'm reminded of a story from the early 1900s about a little boy who killed one of the family geese by throwing a stone and hitting it squarely on the head. Figuring his parents wouldn't notice that one of the twenty-four birds was missing, he buried the dead fowl. But that evening his sister called him aside and said, "I saw what you did. If you don't offer to do the dishes tonight, I'll tell Mother." The next morning she gave him the same warning. All that day and the next the frightened boy felt bound to do the dishes. The following morning, however, he surprised his sister by telling her it was her turn. When she quietly reminded him of what she could do, he replied, "I've already told Mother, and she has forgiven me. Now you do the dishes. I'm free again!"

Guilt is worry that is rooted in fear. We are afraid that God is angry, or that what we have done wrong is too big and too bad, even for God to forgive. We feel we don't deserve forgiveness so we won't receive it. We worry about what people think of our past sins. We are afraid they will never forgive us or see us as good people again. Guilt has everything to do with the past and it has the power to ruin your future. Get over it!

God holds nothing against you if you are sincerely sorry for what you have done and are trusting in the blood of Jesus to cleanse you from your former wickedness. The minute you repent, God forgives and forgets it, so why not follow His example and receive His forgiveness and forget it yourself?

A confident woman does not live in the past, she lets go of it and looks to the future. I believe that many women reading this book have a decision to make right now. Maybe you failed someone, or had an abortion, or committed adultery, stole something, lied or did any number of terrible things. But, God's question to you is what are you going to do today? Will you live the rest of your life serving God and following His plan for you? If you are ready to make that commitment there is nothing in your past that has enough power to hold you back.

Is Dread Draining Your Joy?

People dread many things and most of them don't even realize what dread does to them. It sucks the joy right out of the present moment. The life God has provided for us through Jesus Christ is a precious gift and we should enjoy every moment of it.

Once I was getting a facial and enjoying it extremely. I glanced at the door and saw my clothes hanging on the hook and thought, "Oh, I dread getting up and putting on my clothes and driving all the way home." Then I realized I was letting dread do its dirty work again. It was stealing the joy of the present moment.

Pray and ask God to show you every time you begin to dread any task or something lurking in your future that you're not quite sure of. Merely eliminating dread from your life will release more of your God-given confidence and help you experience more joy.

How often do you find yourself putting things off that you dread doing? Maybe it's that stack of laundry, or those bills that need paying, or worse, maybe it's your annual taxes! Train yourself not to dread unpleasant tasks but to actually tackle them first. The sooner in the day you do the things you don't prefer doing, the more energy you have to do them with. If you wait until the end of the day when most of your energy is gone and then try to do something you really don't like doing, it will be worse than doing it earlier. Dread causes us to procrastinate, but if you're ever going to do something, now is the best time!

Putting something off does not make it go away, it only allows more time to torment you. You can dread or you can confidently take action. As Christians with the power of the Holy Spirit inside of us, surely we can manage to do an unpleasant task without dreading it and with a good attitude. God's power is not available just to make unpleasant things in our lives go away, it is frequently available to walk us through them courageously.

Don't Sweat the Small Stuff

It is highly probable that you dread more little things than you do major things. First of all we have a lot of little things we deal with all the time but the major things come fewer and farther in between. As I began to examine this area of dread in my own life I realized it operated in little daily areas like going to the grocery store, doing laundry, running an errand, or looking for a parking place in a crowded shopping mall. I dreaded waiting because historically, I have not been an extremely patient person. Waiting in lines, traffic, or for slow people to get a job done were things I dreaded and allowed those things to frustrate me.

Like many of you, I have a lot to do and I don't like wasting my time waiting for people and things. But, thank God, I have learned it does no good at all to dread something I have to do anyway. It steals my current joy and I have lost enough of that in my life so I am not willing to give up any more of it. Do you feel that way? Have you also wasted a lot of your life in fear, worry or dread simply because you did not have enough knowledge to know how to deal with it? If so, I believe those days are coming to an end for you. I have faith that the knowledge contained in this book will enable you to enjoy a different quality of life than you previously did.

A conference was being held at a church in Omaha where those in attendance were given helium-filled balloons and told to release them at some point in the service when they felt like expressing the joy in their hearts. All through the service balloons ascended, but when it was over, one-third of the balloons were still unreleased. Let your balloon go.[2] Let your joy be known, even in the little things.

It has become a game with me to try to beat the joy sucker of dread at his own game. I want to prove to the devil that I can enjoy everything I do and that his tactics to steal my joy just won't work anymore. Greater is He that is in me than he that is in the world (1 John 4:4). I believe it glorifies God when we refuse to live in fear, worry, dread or any other relatives of theirs.

When I find myself in a situation I would rather not be in, whether it is waiting or doing an unpleasant task, I make a decision that I will do it joyfully and not dread it and then I exercise self-control. I use those faith muscles that God has given to me as well as every person on the planet. If we allow fear in our lives it breeds more fear, but if we practice walking in faith it becomes easier to do it again and again.

Anointed to Do Natural Things with Supernatural Power

When I think of the word anointed, I think of something being rubbed all over. We are anointed (rubbed all over) with God's power. He has anointed us with the presence and power of the Holy Spirit to help us live life in a supernatural way.

Even as spiritual people we must deal with ordinary natural things all the time. Don't let the things that defeat other people defeat you. Don't faint in your mind when you look at a job that needs to be done and give up before you ever get started. Remember that messes are made a little bit at a time over a long period of time and it will take time to clean them up. Think about how messy your closet, garage or basement is—it didn't get that way overnight and it probably won't get cleaned up without some time and effort. Does a messy area of your home aggravate you every time you see it, yet you put off cleaning it up because you dread it? If so, it is time for change. I want you to attack those messes boldly and have the confidence that you can have order in your

> Dread is expecting something unpleasant to happen and it has nothing to do with faith. Faith looks forward to something good.

life and home. Don't let a messy closet defeat you. You have the power of God in your life. You are able to clean up closets, basements, garages and anything else in your life that is a mess and do it with joy!

Does the thought of mowing the lawn get you discouraged? Do you think, "Oh man, I wish I didn't have to mow the lawn today, I really dread it. I wish I could just go shopping or do something fun." If so, you're not abnormal. We are all tempted to think like that, but the good news is God has given you the spirit of self-control and you can choose what you will think about any situation. You can also choose to do what you know is right no matter how you feel at the moment.

Dale Carnegie said, "You can conquer almost any fear if you will only make up your mind to do so. For remember, fear doesn't exist anywhere except in the mind."[3]

> *For God did not give us a spirit of timidity [of cowardice, of craven and cringing and fawning fear], but [He has given us a spirit] of power and of love and of calm and well-balanced mind and discipline and self-control.* (2 Timothy 1:7)

We can conquer worry and fear, and we can also conquer dread. God has given us a spirit of self-control; all we have to do is exercise it and we will experience freedom from fear and dread.

Dread is expecting something unpleasant to happen and it has nothing to do with faith. Faith looks forward to something good. I believe dread is very deceptive. It is so subtle that it is usually imperceptible. Even while writing this chapter, I needed to stop for awhile and pack all my stuff to get ready to leave a friend's condo I was staying in and return to my home in St. Louis, Missouri. I put my computer and resource material away and began packing.

Only a few seconds went by when I realized I was dreading packing up all my things. Here I was writing a chapter in a book encouraging others not to dread and dread was trying to suck me into its misery. Thankfully I recognized it and was able to say, "no way." I am going to enjoy this packing; I will not dread it!

I believe this is a big area that people really need to look out for. The instant you begin to dread something, your joy starts to go and a "down feeling" sets in. Everything about the devil is down. It is all doom and gloom, depressing and discouraging, negative and yucky. Don't dread anything, but instead face everything with courage and believe you can do anything you need to do and do it with a good attitude.

We know that lack of confidence, worry, dread, and other tormenting emotions are rooted in fear. Fear is the source of these problems, but is there anything we can do to help prevent fear?

Learn to Trust

Babies don't worry, and they don't dread things, so why do adults? As babies we are not responsible for anything and everything is taken care of for us. As we mature and begin to take on responsibility we either learn to be confident, placing our trust in God, or we live in fear, worry and dread. We can look to God and trust in His faithfulness and be confident that He will not let us down or disappoint us. If we don't look to God and place our trust in Him then we carry a burden that we were never meant to bear alone.

Now suddenly WE must make sure everything goes right. WE have to figure things out and come up with answers. Worry is simply fear that things won't work out the way we want them to. But the person who trusts in God has confidence that even if things don't work out the way they desire, that God will have a better plan than they had anyway. Confidence believes that all things work together for good for those who love God and are called according to His purpose (Romans 8:28). Confidence in God is absolutely wonderful because it gives you the confidence that God has answers even when you don't.

Trust is confidence, confidence gives us boldness and boldness does not allow fear to hinder its progress. Boldness is action in the face of fear. Babies naturally trust, but as they have experiences in life, sadly, they learn how to fear. They learn that everything and everyone in their life is not stable and that they cannot always be depended on. People and circumstances change. A child may trust that mom and dad will always love each other and be together. But if mom and dad get a divorce the child's world comes crashing in because something they never even conceived could happen did happen.

As a child continues to mature and encounter various disappointing circumstances they either distrust more and more, or they learn how to trust God who never changes and is always faithful. This does not mean that God always does what we expect Him to do or even what we want Him to do, but He is good. Trusting Him brings a supernatural rest into our soul that allows us to enjoy life, and live free from the tyranny of fear.

Search for Knowledge

Our little dog has no responsibilities. She lies around or sleeps, plays, eats, drinks and goes to the bathroom. When anything unusual happens, it frightens her and she begins to get nervous and shake. Once she understands what is going on she begins to calm down.

One night I was lying in bed and heard a noise upstairs. The longer I listened to it the more frightened I became. Finally, shaking from fear, I went upstairs to see what it was. I had to laugh when I discovered it was ice cubes falling in the ice tray from the ice maker. It just happened that the way they were falling was making a noise they did not normally make.

Lack of knowledge causes fear and knowledge removes it.

Let me tell you a true but tragic story: A woman was once walking along a riverbank with her child. Suddenly the child slipped into the river. The mother screamed in terror! She couldn't swim and besides, she was in the latter stages of pregnancy. Finally, somebody heard her screaming and rushed down to the riverbank. The utter tragedy was, when they stepped into those murky waters to retrieve the child, now dead, they found that the water was only waist deep! That mother could have easily saved her child but didn't because of a lack of knowledge.[4]

The mother must have felt terrible because she didn't check to see how deep the water was. But, fear makes us behave irrationally. Between fear of the child drowning and fear of the water she was paralyzed and did nothing. Knowledge could have changed this entire tragic story.

Knowledge will help you have confidence. If you are going for a job interview, make sure you are prepared and have all the knowledge you will need with you to answer questions they may ask you. We live in a world today where knowledge is as close as your computer. Not only can you do online research about the company you're applying with but you can find tips on how to have a successful interview.

Instead of being afraid of something you are not familiar with, familiarize yourself with it. Do some research or ask some questions. It might take a little effort to do so, but it is better than being tormented by fear.

Learn to Think Differently

You can move from pain to power simply by reeducating your mind. The Bible refers to this process as renewing the mind. Simply put, we must learn how to think differently. If you have been taught to fear you can be taught to be bold, courageous and confident.

Rather than allowing fear to prevent your success and joy in life, you can accept that it is a fact of life. Throughout life you will have to either run away from things in fear or face them confidently. Fear has a large shadow, but it is actually very small. When we fear we will suffer, we already suffer the things we fear. Fear brings torment!

Instead of thinking that you cannot do things if you are afraid, make up your mind that you will do whatever you need to do even if you have to do it afraid. Change your thinking about fear. We allow fear to become a monster in our thinking, but it is one that will back down quickly when confronted. Fear is like the school bully. It pushes everyone around until someone finally challenges it.

The renewing of the mind is the most important thing a person needs to do after receiving Jesus Christ as their Savior. Jesus died for our sins and He wants us to enjoy the life He has provided. God's Word teaches us that He has provided a good plan for each person, yet they will never experience it unless they know about it and also know how to access it (Romans 12:2). People perish and their lives are destroyed for a lack of knowledge (Hosea 4:6). Knowledge and understanding is power when applied properly.

Trisha was haunted by an unreasonable fear that her husband Bob would get involved with another woman and leave her. Her fear made her suspicious and she frequently accused her husband of things that made no sense to him at all. For example, if he needed to work overtime she would call his office to check and make sure he was there because she suspected he was seeing another woman. If for some reason he did not answer the phone she panicked. She would even get into her car and drive past his place of work just to make sure he was there.

One night she called to check on him and when he did not answer she drove to his office. He was in the bathroom when she called and he immediately left to go home after that. By the time she arrived at his office his car was gone and the little voice inside her head began tormenting her with accusations against Bob. She was surprised to find his car in the garage, but it was too late to gain control of her emotions, she was already enraged with anger and suspicion. When she approached Bob, she was saying so many things that made no sense at all to him that he began to wonder about her sanity. This scene and others like it were slowly but surely eroding Bob's respect for Trisha.

Once he bought her a special bracelet to surprise her. They were planning to go to dinner that weekend and he had hidden the bracelet. In the middle of the week while cleaning out a drawer she normally would not get into, she found the bracelet and once again, because of her fear, she immediately thought that it was a gift he had purchased for another woman. It never entered her mind that it might be a gift for her. It is not the nature of fear to look at the positive possibilities, but instead it always assumes the worst.

Even when Bob told her that he had purchased it for her, she didn't believe him at first. Trisha's behavior began to seriously affect their relationship and he told her that she had to get to the bottom of these ridiculous fears. He never gave her one reason to distrust him and could not understand what her problem was. To be honest, she didn't understand it either until she began to pray about it. God revealed to her that her fear was the fruit of a sudden and tragic change in her own life when as a child her father left her mother for another woman who he worked with.

Having understanding about where the fear came from really helped Trisha to resist it. She began reading and educating herself about the nature of fear. For quite some time she still had some of the same thoughts and feelings but she was now able to reason with herself because she had knowledge. As time went by the fear went with it and Bob and Trisha's relationship healed.

Many fears are the result of something that happened in the past and that we fear will happen again. If a person's mother died of cancer they might fall prey to a fear that they will die the same way. They could become paranoid and fear that every little ache,

> When we lean into the dilemma and trust the hand of God—we gain control.

pain or strange feeling in their body is cancer. Fear that you will suffer, causes suffering already while you are in fear. The fear we have about an event that may happen is usually worse than the thing would be even if it did happen. Don't be afraid that your life will end; instead, believe that it's just beginning.

Instead of fighting a fear or merely putting up with it, start praying about how it gained entrance into your life, especially if the fear is a repetitive one. I always became fearful when Dave tried to correct our children and it was because I was corrected in an abusive way when I was growing up at home. I didn't understand the reason for my fear until God revealed it to me through prayer. You might even need to get some counseling to get to the root of your fears, but whatever you do, don't just put up with them. God has a great life waiting for you and you must reach for it confidently.

John Ortberg tells the story of a snow skier who after pointing his ski tips down the barrel of a black-rated slope, quickly entered the land of no control and instinctively leaned backward in hope of reversing sure disaster. "We all do that," says Ortberg. "But in life, as in snow-skiing, the answer is not to react in fear and lean back and away from the experience, but rather lean into it. When we lean into the dilemma and trust the hand of God—we gain control. Fear is a snare!"[5]

Remember not to run from your fears, lean into them and you will conquer them.

Poor Training

Parents, teachers and other role models can teach children how to fear or they can teach them to be bold. A mother who is fearful herself will transmit that fear to her children. She will be overly cautious about many things and a silent fear sinks into the heart of her children. We should not teach our children to live recklessly, but we should teach them to be bold, take action, and to never be so afraid of making mistakes that they won't try things. I believe we should teach our children and those under our authority to take chances in life. If we never take a chance we will never make progress. Progress always requires stepping into the unknown. Experience gives us confidence but we never get experience unless we step out and try things we have not tried before.

A child who is told over and over, "you better not try that, you might get hurt," will more than likely develop a deep rooted fear of trying new things. If a child hears "be careful" too frequently they may learn to be so careful that they end up living a narrow life that has no room for adventure. I encourage you to teach others by word and example how to be bold and courageous. Tell people to try things, reminding them that making a mistake is not the worst thing that can happen.

What Does the Future Hold?

None of us knows for sure what the future holds. This lack of knowledge often opens the door for fear. What if I become disabled? What if my spouse dies? What if my child dies? What if we have another world war? What about terrorism? What kind of world will I be living in twenty-five years from now? Wondering about things we don't have answers to opens the door to fear. Instead of wondering, trust God that whatever your future holds He will enable you to handle it when the time comes. Wherever you are going, God has already been there and paved the way for you.

I look at some of the things people go through and I think to myself, "I am afraid I could never go through that with the graciousness and courage I have seen them display." Then I remind myself that when we must go through something, God gives us the strength to do so. When we merely fear going through some-thing, we do it without any help from God at all. When I look back over my life and remember some of the things God has brought me through I think, "how did I do that?" It was because of God's grace and power. He enabled me to do what I needed to do at the time and He will always do the same thing for you if you ask Him to. We may not know the future, but if we know the One who holds the future in His hands, we can look forward to it expec-tantly and without fear. If God brings you to it, He will bring you through it.

Chapter Thirteen

THE RELATIONSHIP BETWEEN STRESS AND FEAR

Stress is one of the biggest problems we face in our society today. Everything is so fast-paced, loud and excessive that our mental, emotional and physical systems stay on overload. We are inundated with information. We have newspapers, magazines and 24-hour news networks that don't just reach us through our television but through our cell phones and other mobile devices. At one time, a popular Web search engine indexed more than 3,307,998,701 Web pages![1] It's hard enough to think about that number, let alone the content that goes with it. We have information overload and it is no wonder we have trouble calming our minds down so we can rest. In addition to what the world throws at us, we have schedules that are insane. There are never enough hours in any day to get everything done we are trying to do. We hurry and we rush, we feel frustrated and tired and we're the first to say, "I'm under so much stress that I feel I am going to explode."

Could fear be the root of many of our stresses? I believe it is. I believe we often get involved in things just because we are afraid of being left out. We are afraid we won't know what is going on or that someone else will gain control of a situation if we are not there to speak for ourselves. We are afraid they might criticize us or think poorly of us if we say we don't want to be involved.

We want our children to be like all the other children, so we let them get involved in far too many things and most of them require some involvement from us also. We are afraid they will get rejected, especially if we experienced a lot of rejection when we were children.

I never felt that I fit in as a child or teenager. Because of the abuse in my home and all the secrets I had to keep I could not develop proper relationships. I had to say no to a lot of invitations just because my father was so terribly strict and the result was that people stopped asking. I always felt left out and a bit odd.

I was afraid my children would go through the same pain I did so anything they wanted to do I thought we should find a way to do it, lest they feel left out as I did. People get under financial stress trying to have what everyone else has. Have you been one of the moms who bought a $150.00 pair of tennis shoes that you could not afford for your child just because "everyone has them?"

Are you so afraid of displeasing people that you say "yes" to a lot of things you know you should be saying "no," to? If so, your stress is not caused by all the things you have to do, it is because you are afraid of disapproval.

We are afraid to be different so we desperately try to keep up with all the other people in our lives and it wears us out. The truth is we just want to go home and sit in a chair but we don't want people to think we are a dud so we keep pushing ourselves to do things we don't want to do.

Take a minute to stop and look closely at the reasons you are doing the things you currently do. If any of them are being done out of fear, then eliminate them. You will be amazed at how much time you may have if you have a spirit-led schedule rather than a people-driven one.

Confident People Do More with Less Stress

You might ask, "Doesn't a really confident person get involved in a lot of things?" Yes, they probably do, but it isn't because of fear.

Whatever they are involved in they are confident they should be involved in. When we do things out of desire and confidence, they affect us totally different than when we do them out of wrong motives and fear. God will not energize our fears, but He does energize us if we have faith that we are doing the right thing and approach a project with confidence in Him.

Fear drains you of whatever energy you might have had and leaves you feeling stressed to the max, when confidence and faith actually energizes you. A confident person can do more with less stress because they live with an ease that fearful people never experience.

I don't believe that what we do creates stress nearly as much as how we do it. If we do something fearfully and under pressure with no real desire to do it, then stress and no joy is the result. You're miserable. If you have been under a lot of stress lately I encourage you to take an honest inventory of not only what you are doing, but why you are doing it. If fear is the reason you're involved then eliminate some stress by getting your priorities straight. Your priority is not to keep everyone else in your life happy by doing all the things they expect; it is to live a life that is pleasing to God and one that you can enjoy.

Too many people are not living their dreams because they are living their fears. In other words, instead of doing things out of their heart, they do them because they are afraid of what will happen if they don't. Someone will get angry! I will get left out! People will talk about me! It is time that you started being the person you really want to be. It is time to reach for your dreams. What has God placed in your heart? Is there something you want to do that you have been waiting on? I believe God's timing is very important and I certainly don't think we should take action foolishly, but some people never do anything but "wait" all of their lives. They wait for something to happen when they should be making something happen.

When people are frustrated and feel unfulfilled it creates stress.

Too many people are not living their dreams because they are living their fears.

There is nothing more stressful than going through the motions everyday and still feeling at the end of each day, week, month and year that you are no closer than you ever were to reaching your dream or goal. God has created us to bear good fruit. He said, "Be fruitful and multiply." If we are not doing that we will feel frustrated.

Playing It Safe

Some people never realize the fulfillment of their dreams because they always play it safe. Although safety is necessary, too much of it is merely another manifestation of fear.

A farmer was once sitting on his front porch when a friend dropped by to visit.

"How's your wheat going this year?" asked the visitor.

"Ain't got any," replied the farmer. "I didn't plant any. I'm afraid the weevil will get into it and ruin me."

"Oh, well how's your corn?"

"Ain't got any," replied the farmer. "I didn't plant any. I'm afraid the crows will eat it all up and ruin me."

"Oh, well how are your potatoes going?"

"Ain't got any," replied the farmer. "I didn't plant any. I'm afraid the tater bugs will poison them and ruin me."

"Well, what did you plant this year?" asked the confused visitor.

"Nutin'," replied the farmer. "I just played it safe."

Think of all of the products and services we would miss out on if their creators had decided to "play it safe" instead of pursuing their dreams. What if Henry Ford had simply been content to run a sawmill instead of going on to pursue being an engineer and ultimately one of our nation's first automobile creators?[2] What if Alexander Graham Bell had listened to his friends and family and focused on the telegraph instead of his telephone invention? What if Jonas Salk, the scientist who discovered the vaccine for polio, had followed his initial "safe" inclination to go into law instead of medical research?[3]

Always living in the safe zone of life and never taking chances actually makes one a thief and a robber. You might think that statement is a bit strong but the truth is always strong, and the truth also makes us free. If I spend my life keeping myself safe then I rob everyone else of my gifts and talents simply because I am too afraid to step out and be willing to find out what I can do in life. I have a feeling that some of my readers have not even begun to live yet and NOW is the time for you to stop "playing it safe" and start being bold and courageous.

Inactivity Breeds Tiredness and Stress

Too much activity and no rest definitely is the culprit behind most stress, but no activity is also a problem. I am sure you have heard that exercise is a great stress reliever and it is very true. I would rather be physically tired from exercise and movement than tired in my soul from doing nothing and being bored.

I have noticed if I sit in a chair too long I will feel extremely tired when I get up. Why? God gave us all the joints in our body because He expected us to move! Movement means I am alive.

The Bible clearly warns against the dangers of laziness (Proverbs 12:27, 2 Thessalonians 3:6–10). The lazy man has nothing and he gets exactly what he deserves which is nothing. If you give things to a lazy man or woman they won't take care of them and you'll notice that everything around them is in shambles. Their car (if they have one) is dirty. Their house (if they have one) is messy and dirty. They are often in debt. People who are lazy spend their life "wishing" that something good would happen to them. They want others to do for them what they should be doing for themselves. They are miserable human beings and their lives bear no good fruit.

Work is good for all of us. As a matter of fact, God said we should work six days and rest one. That shows how important work and activity are in God's eyes. God has created us to work, not to sit idly by and do nothing. Perhaps some of you are at a place in life where you simply need to "get up and get going." There are several good stories in the Bible about people who had serious problems and when they asked Jesus for help He told them to "GET UP!"

In the fifth chapter of John we see one example. A man was crippled and he lay by the pool of Bethesda for thirty-eight years waiting for his miracle. When Jesus came to the man and asked him how long he had been in that condition, the man gave the length of time and then continued to tell Jesus how he had nobody to put him into the pool at the right time and how others always got ahead of him. Jesus told the man to "GET UP, PICK UP YOUR BED AND WALK!" (John 5:8). The man felt sorry for himself so he just lay there and did nothing. The answer to his problem surfaced when he made an effort to move.

Are you sick and tired of being sick and tired? Well, don't be like the story of the old mountaineer and his wife who were sitting in front of the fireplace one evening just whiling away the time. After a long silence, the wife said: "Jed, I think it's raining. Get up and go outside and see."

The old mountaineer continued to gaze into the fire for a second, sighed, then said, "Aw, Ma, why don't we just call in the dog and see if he's wet."[4]

GET UP and start doing whatever you can do to get the messes in your life cleaned up. If they are marriage messes then do your part. Don't worry about what your spouse is not doing, just do your part and God will reward you. If you have a financial mess, then stop spending and start paying off your debts. Get an extra job for a period of time if you need to. If you are not able to do that then ask God to show you what you can do. Remember, you cannot have a harvest without first sowing seed of some kind. Remember what I've already said: "If you do what you can do, then God will do what you cannot do."

A lot of laziness is rooted in fear. People are so afraid to do something that they form a habit of doing nothing. They sit idly by and become jealous of the people who have the life they would like to have. They become resentful because things never work out for them. They fail to realize that "Things cannot work out for them if they don't work!"

Only Change Will Relieve Stress

If you are stressed out all the time something will have to change in order for the stress to be relieved. It will not just go away as long as you keep doing the same thing. We cannot expect to keep doing the same thing over and over and get a different result. If you want different results, you have to change the ingredients.

Now, as soon as I mentioned the word "change" some of you tensed up because you are afraid of change. Almost one hundred years ago, the clerk of Abbington Presbytery came up with percentages for the kinds of attitudes people have about change and I think they still apply today.

1. Early innovators (2.6%), run with new ideas
2. Early adaptors (13.4%), influenced by (1) but not initiators
3. Slow Majority (34%), the herd-followers
4. Reluctant Majority (34%)
5. Antagonistic (16%), they will never change[5]

If you're like the bottom 84% of people in the above list, you don't like change, and you want the safety of sameness. It is amazing to me how some people spend their lives resisting change

Take some bold steps of faith and change anything the Lord leads you to change.

while others thrive on it. Change keeps life fresh and adventurous.

Take some bold steps of faith and change anything the Lord leads you to change. If what you are doing with your time is not bearing good fruit, then make a change. If you are not getting enough rest, make a change. If you are not disciplining your children and their behavior is causing you a lot of stress, then make a change. If you are not taking care of yourself, then make a change. If you are bored, make a change. If your friends are taking advantage of you, then make a change! Are you getting the point? Stress can be relieved if you're not afraid to make changes.

You may be afraid of change but it is also possible that even if you find the courage to make the necessary changes that other people in your life won't like the changes you make. Don't be afraid of them either. You will get used to the changes and so will they. If you don't take action now you will still be complaining about the same things a year from now, and a year after that, and ten years after that, and there will be no end to your misery. The time is NOW! Boldness takes action, but fear breeds inactivity and procrastination. The choice is yours!

Chapter Fourteen

CHOOSING BOLDNESS

Maybe you've stayed with me this far and you're still thinking to yourself, "Joyce, I'm a timid and shy person, that's just my nature. I just don't think I can change." You may feel timid and shy but you can choose to walk boldly through life. The main thing I want you to remember is that you can feel afraid, you can feel timid, you can feel downright cowardly and yet you can make the choice to walk boldly and as if fear did not exist! Your free will is stronger than your feelings if you will exercise it. You may be like thousands of others who have catered to your feelings for so long that they now control you. Your will, like a muscle, becomes weak if not exercised. As you begin to ask God to help you and exercise your willpower against your feelings, it will get easier and easier to be the person you truly want to be, the person God has designed you to be.

When I think of what boldness looks like on someone, I think of someone who is daring, courageous, brave, and fearless. Some people think they are bold but they are merely rude, forward and impudent. They would be much better off to be honest and admit being afraid but keep going, rather than try and pretend to be brave while living a lie.

I must admit, that's how I was for many years of my life. I thought I was a bold woman, but the truth is I was very fearful. I was not facing my fears, and I was pretending to myself and the rest of the world that I was not afraid of anything. There is a difference between truly facing fear and just ignoring it and pretending

When I think of what boldness looks like on someone, I think of someone who is daring, courageous, brave, and fearless.

you are not afraid and covering your fear with a phony boldness that is merely rude and impudent.

I was quick to speak my mind but what I said was often foolish and inappropriate. I took control of situations thinking I would step out in boldness and do something since nobody else seemed to be doing anything, only to later realize that I had taken authority that was not mine to take.

I frequently moved impatiently and too quickly, once again thinking I was bold, but I made many mistakes and hurt a lot of people because I did not take time to seek wisdom. I was really very immature and didn't know anything about true boldness.

If anyone offended or insulted me I was quick to defend myself and "put them in their place." I made it clear that I would not be mistreated. However, as I became a student of God's Word in an effort to straighten out a very messed up life, I was corrected by Scriptures like:

A fool's wrath is quickly and openly known, but a prudent man ignores an insult. (Proverbs 12:16)

Beloved, never avenge yourselves, but leave the way open for [God's] wrath; for it is written, Vengeance is Mine, I will repay [requite] says the Lord. (Romans 12:19)

It takes true courage and boldness to walk in faith and wait for God to vindicate you when you are ill treated. What I thought was boldness had no ability to do that. A true person would be much better off to tell the truth and say, "I'm afraid but I'm going to do it afraid," than to pretend they were not afraid and live in phoniness and self-deception. Genuinely brave people not only have the courage to take action, they also have the courage to wait when they need to.

A Man's Mind Plans His Way

I always had a plan and was always quick to execute it, but many of my plans still failed. Proverbs 16: 9 tells us that a man's mind plans his way, but his steps are made sure and accurate only by the Lord. Proverbs says many wise things that we would do well to listen to. It also tells us that pride goes before destruction, and a haughty spirit before a fall (Proverbs 16:18). Many people think they are bold, but they are merely proud and arrogant. They think too highly of themselves and always end up looking down on other people and hurting them.

My plans always worked everything out in my favor without seriously considering other people's needs, but God's plans give forethought to everyone's needs. We must learn to wait for God's plans to develop. He perfects everything that concerns us. True boldness moves in God's timing, it moves at the right time.

During the three years of Jesus' earthly ministry people thought He was crazy. His own brothers were embarrassed by Him and in an effort to save their reputation they told Him He needed to go somewhere else and do His works. If He was unwilling to do that, they had another option for Him. They told Him to take action and stop doing His works in secret. They tried to convince Him it was time to show Himself and His works to the world. In other words, they wanted Jesus to impress the people with what He could do.

He responded to them by saying, "My time (opportunity) has not come yet . . ." (John 7:6).

How many of us could show that type of self-control? If you could do the miracles that He could do and were being made fun of and challenged to show your stuff, what would you do? Would you wait until you absolutely knew that it was the right time or would you take action that was not sanctioned by God?

It is good to have plans and I believe we should plan boldly and aggressively, but we must be wise enough to know that our plans will ultimately fail without God.

Except the Lord builds the house, they labor in vain that build it. (Psalm 127:1)

We can build without God as our foundation but like any building without a strong foundation, we will eventually fall.

The Foolishness of Self-Confidence

Since I am writing a book on how you can become a confident woman I want to state again as I did earlier in the book that I am not talking about self-confidence. I don't want you to have confidence in yourself unless that confidence is first rooted in God. If our confidence is a fruit of us being first rooted in God then we have the right kind of confidence which produces true boldness.

As Paul said, "we are self-confident in His confidence."

Those of us who think we are bold should ask ourselves if we have confidence or conceit. Bill Crawford said, "The difference between self-confidence and conceit is as simple as love and fear. Jesus was self-confident . . . Hitler was afraid."

When I am teaching on confidence, people often express concerns about the difference between self-confidence and conceit. They say that they have been taught not to say (or even think) positive things about themselves. If they did, it would sound self-centered and selfish. Good parents teach their children not to brag, and it is right to do so. No one enjoys a braggart who is in love with herself and believes she is the answer to all of humanities problems. Some people think they know so much that it is obvious they know nothing at all. We have not even begun to have knowledge until we know that we don't know anything compared to what we need to know.

In teaching our children not to brag we should not teach them that it is wrong to acknowledge the positive aspects of who they are. If you go and apply for a job but due to fear of sounding self-conceited you understate your skills, you probably won't get the job. Be confident, but let your confidence be rooted in God. We are what we are due to His grace and mercy.

> Take each compliment that you receive as a rose and at the end of the day take the entire bouquet and offer it back to God, knowing that it came from Him.

Confidence breeds confidence. When someone presents themselves in a confident manner it causes me to have confidence that they can do what needs to be done. They don't necessarily have to keep repeating to me that they know they are nothing without God, but they should tell Him regularly.

I remember complimenting a friend on doing a fine job of grilling for a dinner party. He was a very godly man and immediately responded that it was not him but the Lord. In my opinion, it would have been much better if he had said, "thank you for the compliment," and in his own prayer time thanked God for helping him. When someone compliments us we should graciously receive it. Take each compliment that you receive as a rose and at the end of the day take the entire bouquet and offer it back to God, knowing that it came from Him.

The book of Proverbs has much to say about self-confidence and spares no words in stating that only a fool is self-confident.

> Like snow in summer and like rain in harvest, so honor is not fitting for a [self-confident] fool. (Proverbs 26:1)

A fool is always taking some kind of beating from the devil because he opens the door through self-confidence. God is our defense and protection but our confidence must be in Him and not in us. When we are wholly trusting in God for all of our strength in all the affairs of life, we experience a divine protection that is amazing.

The self-confident man or woman may experience a financial

beating. They make bad deals, get cheated, invest in stocks that become worthless and all because they moved in their own knowledge rather than seeking the wisdom of God.

The fool may experience a mental beating. The self-confident person must worry, reason, be anxious and have fear. They depend on themselves to solve their problems so they have to figure things out.

Fools also experience emotional beating. Nothing really works out right when people lean on themselves. They always end up being upset because their plans do not work. They spend most of their time frustrated. Nothing is more frustrating than doing your very best to solve problems and yet always failing. We begin to think something is wrong with us and God is merely hindering our success in the hopes that we will eventually wear ourselves out and come to Him for help.

If I were to paraphrase 1 Peter 5:5 in the Bible, it would say, "All of you should put on humility. Wear it as a garment and never let it be stripped from you. Live with freedom from pride and arrogance toward one another because God sets Himself against the proud and haughty (the presumptuous and boastful) and He opposes and even frustrates and defeats them but He helps the humble."

Overestimating yourself and not seeing yourself as you really are without God causes a chain reaction of problems. It causes high-mindedness, exclusivity, an inability to adjust and adapt to others; inability to get along with people . . . basically because in their high-mindedness they fail to see their own flaws which prevents them from bearing with other people's flaws.

Is It Possible to Be Humble and Bold?

Not only is it possible to be humble and bold, it is impossible to be truly bold without humility. Joshua was a man who was both. God told him to finish the job Moses started and take the Israelites into the Promised Land. Immediately after giving Joshua the command, God announced that He would be with him the same as He was with Moses (Joshua 1:5).

Joshua's confidence rested in the fact that God was with Him and because of that he was able to go forward to do something that he probably felt unqualified to do. Joshua must have felt fear because the Lord repeatedly told him to "fear not," which means "don't run!"

God told Joshua that if he would be strong, confident and full of courage that he would cause the people to inherit the land which God had promised them.

> *No man shall be able to stand before you all the days of your life. As I was with Moses, so I will be with you; I will not fail you or forsake you.*
>
> *Be strong [confident] and of a good courage, for you shall cause this people to inherit the land which I swore to their fathers to give them.*
>
> *Only you be strong and very courageous, that you may do according to all the law which Moses My servant commanded you. Turn not from it to the right hand or to the left, that you may prosper wherever you go.* (Joshua 1:5–7)

Notice the emphasis that God places on Himself. Joshua was to keep his eyes on God and His command. He was not to get entangled in other things that might frighten him, he was to stay focused on his goal. If he obeyed God he would not only help himself, he would also have the privilege of leading multitudes of people into a better life.

And just in case he needed one last encouragement God basically repeats Himself in Joshua 1:9 saying,

> *Have not I commanded you? Be strong, vigorous, and very courageous. Be not afraid, neither be dismayed, for the Lord your God is with you wherever you go.*

I believe God's discourse to Joshua is evidence that there would be reasons in the natural for him to fear and become dismayed and want to turn back. When we take steps of faith to make progress in life there is no guarantee that we will not experience opposition. But we do have God's guarantee that He will always be with us and that is truly all we need. We don't need to know what God is going to do, how He is going to do it, or when He is going to do it. We only need to know that He is with us.

Be Not Afraid

Jeremiah was a very young man who was given a very big job. God told him that he had been called as a prophet to the nations. He was to be a mouthpiece for God. The thoughts of it frightened Jeremiah and he began to make all kinds of excuses about why he could not do what God was asking. He was looking at himself and he needed to look at God. He was also looking at people and wondering what they would think and do if he took the bold step God was encouraging him to take.

In answer to Jeremiah's fearful comments God told him to stop talking and just go do what He was telling him to do. God said, "be not afraid of them (their faces) for I am with you to deliver you" (Jeremiah 1:8). Jeremiah gets the same speech that Joshua got. Don't look at the circumstances: just remember that I am with you and that is all you need.

Jeremiah was feeling the same fear that one little five-year-old boy experienced the day his mother asked him to go into the kitchen pantry and get her a can of tomato soup. He didn't want to go in alone. "It's dark in there and I'm scared." She asked again, and he persisted. Finally she said, "It's okay—Jesus will be in there with you." Johnny walked hesitantly to the door and slowly opened it. He peeked inside, saw it was dark, and started to leave when all at once an idea came, and he said: "Jesus, if you're in there, would you hand me that can of tomato soup?"[1]

Toward the end of Jeremiah 1, God tells the prophet that if he continues to be afraid (running instead of confronting) that He would permit him to be overcome. Remember that God wants us to face things, and not run from them. Whatever you run from will always be waiting for you somewhere else. Our strength to conquer is found in pressing forward with God. The Lord told Jeremiah in the final verse of chapter one that the people would fight against him but they would not prevail for one simple reason . . . "I am with you."

It is interesting to note that Jeremiah was warned that there would be a fight, but even in that, he was not to be afraid because in the end he would have the victory.

Phony Boldness Exchanged for the Real Thing

The Apostle Peter was a man who began with phony boldness. He thought he was bold but in reality, he was forward, presumptuous, rude and foolish on many occasions. Peter was usually the first one to speak but what he said was often prideful and completely out of place. Peter thought more highly of himself than he should have. He needed to trade his self-confidence for confidence in God.

Jesus tried to warn Peter that he would deny Him three times in a very short period of time but Peter thought that was absolutely impossible. After Jesus allowed Himself to be captured, Peter was recognized as one of His disciples. He immediately denied that he even knew Him. Peter continued on in the same fearful response until he quickly denied Christ three times. Peter, who appeared to be so bold, literally fell apart in fear during a real crisis (Luke 22).

Jesus promised His disciples that after His death and resurrection He would send His Holy Spirit to fill them with real power.

They would experience true boldness that would be rooted and grounded in their faith in Him. Peter, along with others, received this power from on high on the day of Pentecost and Acts 1 finds Peter preaching boldly in the streets of Jerusalem, no longer caring one bit about what anyone thought. Peter saw himself for the pretender and sinner that he was. He repented, was forgiven and was filled with holy boldness that can come only from God.

What Are You Facing?

We have looked at the challenging circumstances of Joshua, Jeremiah and Peter, but what are you facing right now? Are there threatening circumstances looming in front of you? If so, remember that God is with you and He will never leave you or forsake you. Ask Him to help you and He will. You don't have to pretend to be brave; if you are frightened, tell God how you feel. If you are worried, give those worries to God. After all, He knows anyway. You can say you feel fear, but I also encourage you to say that you won't let it stop you from going forward. I challenge you to say, "I feel fear, but I choose boldness!"

Chapter Fifteen

WINNERS NEVER QUIT

Quitting is not an option for the confident woman. She must decide what she wants or needs to do and make her mind up that she will finish her course. You will experience some opposition no matter what you attempt to do in life. The Apostle Paul said that when doors of opportunity opened to him, opposition often came with it (1 Corinthians 16:9). Confidence believes that it can handle whatever comes its way; it doesn't fear what has not happened yet.

I still remember the first Sunday morning I ministered at a church we started in the inner city of St. Louis. Our goal was to help the hurting people in that area and give them hope. I stood in the pulpit that day and announced loudly, "I am here to stay." I knew others who had tried to do similar works and, after a period of time, gave up. I made up my mind when I started that I would finish.

We have endured opposition. Local churches got upset because a new church was coming into the area. They were afraid that we would take their congregations. Their comment was, "We don't need a big ministry coming in here and taking our people." Attitudes such as that are fear-based and foolish.

One of our staff members was injured in a drive-by shooting, but we still didn't leave and neither did he.

Occasionally, members of the congregation had windows broken in their cars during the church service, but they did not leave. A couple of times cars were even stolen, but we still stayed.

The pastor was caught in an affair with another employee and we became more determined than ever. We said, "Even if we have to start all over, we are not going to leave." Fear said, "the people in the congregation will leave when they here this." I said, "If anyone leaves, God will send two more to replace them." I addressed the congregation and openly shared the truth with them. I told them we would get someone good to pastor the church, that Satan wanted to use the situation to divide the church, but we weren't going to let that happen. People really appreciated the honesty and no one left. The church has grown and is one thousand members strong at this time.

When you attempt to do something and fear rears its ugly head, you must remember that the whole goal of fear is to stop you. Fear wants you to run, to withdraw and to hide. God wants you to finish what you began.

The Apostle Paul was given a job to do and he was determined to do it even though he knew that it meant imprisonment and suffering. He kept his eyes on the finish line, not on what he knew he would go through. He said he wasn't moved by the opposition, but that his goal was to finish his course with joy. Paul not only wanted to finish what he started, he wanted to enjoy the journey. Enjoyment is not possible if we are afraid all the time. Fear brings present torment concerning future situations that may not happen anyway. Paul knew that whatever did happen, God would be faithful to strengthen him so that he might patiently endure it.

Be Careful What You Look At

If we stare at our giants too much, the fear of them will overtake us. Keep your eyes on the prize, not the pain. In the Bible, Paul explains how they were pressed on every side and troubled and oppressed in every way. They could see no way out but they refused to give up. He explains in 2 Corinthians 4:9 how they were persecuted but not deserted or left by God to stand alone. Paul said, "We are struck down to the ground, but never struck out and destroyed." I can feel my heart being stirred with courage even as I listen to Paul. He

> If we stare at our problems too much, think and talk about them too much, they are likely to defeat us. Glance at your problems but stare at Jesus.

made his mind up that no matter what happened he was going to finish his course. Paul explained that they did not get discouraged (utterly spiritless, exhausted, and wearied out through fear) because they looked not at the things they could see but to the things they could not see. (2 Corinthians 4:8, 9, 16, 18).

If we stare at our problems too much, think and talk about them too much, they are likely to defeat us. Glance at your problems but stare at Jesus. We don't deny the existence of problems, we don't ignore them, but we do not permit them to rule us. Any problem you have is subject to change. All things are possible with God!

When David came against the giant Goliath, he did not stand for hours looking at the giant wondering how to win the battle. The Bible says that he ran quickly to the battle line, all the time talking about the greatness of God and declaring his victory ahead of time. David did not run away from his giant; he courageously ran toward him.

Robert Schuller said, "If you listen to your fears, you will die never knowing what a great person you might have been."[1]

If David had run from Goliath he would never have been King of Israel. He was anointed by God to be king twenty years before he wore the crown. During those years he faced his giants and proved that he had the tenacity to endure difficulty without quitting.

Did David feel any fear as he approached Goliath? I think he did. In David's writings he never claimed to be free from the feelings of fear. As a matter of fact he talked about being afraid.

What time I am afraid, I will have confidence in and put my trust and reliance in You.

By [the help of] God I will praise His word; on God I lean, rely, and confidently put my trust; I will not fear. What can man, who is flesh, do to me? (Psalm 56:3, 4)

David was clearly saying that even though he *felt* fear, he chose to *be* confident!

Get Up Again

Paul said that we are each running a race and that we should run it to win. Winning requires preparation, training, sacrifice and a willing to press past our opposition. It often requires failing many times but continuing, always keeping going, despite any opposition we may encounter along the way.

In 1921 Peter Kyne wrote a moving story about a man who knew what it meant to never quit. *The Go-Getter* is a story that continues to inspire people today.[2] I'd like to share a short summary of it with you.

Bill Peck comes home from World War I with a limp, no left arm, and a spirit of determination greater than that of ten healthy men put together. After interviewing at the Ricks Logging & Lumbering Company twice and still not getting hired, Bill calls on the founder of the company, Alden Ricks, and urges him to persuade the rest of the management to give Bill a chance.

"I want you to go over [management's] heads and give me a job," Bill tells his prospective employer. "I don't care a hoot what it is, provided I can do it. If I can do it, I'll do it better than it was ever done before, and if I can't do that I'll quit to save you from having to fire me."

Despite his reluctance to interfere in the hiring decisions of the men he has put in charge to run things, Alden is taken with the young veteran. He admires Bill's skill at selling himself, and he is doubly impressed by Bill's easygoing, congenial manner when refusing to take no for an answer. Alden convinces his right-hand man, Mr. Skinner, to hire Bill, with a stern warning to the veteran that he'll receive three chances and no more.

"When do I report for duty, sir?" he asks and starts that afternoon.

But Bill has his work cut out for him. Mr. Skinner, privately advised by Alden Ricks, gives him his assignment: to sell skunk wood, a "coarse and stringy and wet and heavy" lumber that, for a short while after it's cut, "smells just like a skunk." It's a wood that few buy, and Mr. Skinner is sure he'll be letting the new salesman go when he isn't able to sell it. But Bill takes his bottom-of-the-barrel mission in stride and accepts with his typical answer: "It shall be done."

Two months pass and nothing is heard of Bill, who has been sent out into the Utah, Arizona, New Mexico, and Texas territory to see what sales he can scare up for skunk wood. Nothing is heard from Bill—but his orders start pouring in. "Two carloads of larch rustic" for Salt Lake City and "a carload of skunk spruce boards, random lengths and grades, at a dollar above the price given by Skinner" for a retail yard in Ogden—a company that Mr. Skinner has tried to get business from for many years. By the time Bill reaches Texas, his orders for skunk wood are coming in so fast that Mr. Skinner is forced to ask him to turn his attention to selling the better wood, like Douglas fir and redwood.

By the time he returns to the office, Bill has outsold the company's best salesman and even receives a larger salary as a result of his success. Alden Ricks decides that perhaps Bill is worthy of a new test. This is fine with Mr. Skinner, who is certain that Bill will fail and he'll be taken off the payroll for good.

Alden Ricks calls Bill and asks if the young war veteran would mind running an errand for him. Alden has seen a blue vase in the window of a particular store and needs Bill to go purchase it for him so he can take it out of town to his daughter's house that evening for her wedding anniversary.

But the store is not where Alden Ricks said it was. When Bill can't reach Alden on the phone, he searches on foot and finally finds the store several blocks away, closed for the evening. But the name of the owner is on the door, and Bill soon begins a series of phone calls out of the phone book, calling as many B. Jonsens as there are listed. He finally talks to the right one, who connects him with an assistant who meets him at the store.

But the price of the vase is an enormous amount—two thousand dollars—and the assistant refuses to take a check. Determined to make good on his promise, Bill phones Mr. Skinner, who avoids helping in any way. Bill is forced to figure out yet another way to get the vase, putting a special ring of his own down as collateral.

After finally purchasing the vase, he rushes to the train station where he was supposed to meet Alden Ricks. The train left the station several hours earlier, so Bill tracks down a pilot friend who flies him to a point by the railroad track. There Bill sits and waits. When he sees the train approaching, he flags it down with a Sunday paper he has twisted into a torch and lit. He forces the train to stop and convinces the brakeman to allow him to board. Though he is a bit late, he finally delivers the vase to the stateroom of one astonished Alden Ricks, who explains to the exhausted man that the vase was his "supreme test of a go-getter."

"It's a job that many before you have walked away from at the first sign of an obstacle," Alden Ricks says. "You thought you carried into this stateroom a two-thousand-dollar vase, but between ourselves, what you really carried in was a ten-thousand-dollar job as our Shanghai manager."

What a moving story! Doesn't it encourage you? Doesn't it make you want to finish your own challenges in life? What I like best about this story is that Bill could have given up at any point. He could have broken into the store, or he could have just gone home. But he used integrity, resourcefulness, and determination to get the job done. He never gave up. Cowards quit, but confidence and courage finish.

Are you tempted to give up on something right now? Don't! Finishing your challenge will build your confidence. You will trust yourself more, and that is important.

When you always choose the easy way, your conscience is stirred. You may try to ignore it, but your conscience whispers to you that you have not done your best.

So when you are faced with decisions that plague or wear you down, be confident in your ability that you will see success. And repeat what Bill Peck always said: "It shall be done!"

Winners don't always take first place, but they must finish the race. Are you tempted to give up on something right now? Don't! Finishing your race will build your confidence. You will trust yourself more and that is important. When we make decisions that we know inside our heart aren't the best decisions, it bothers our conscience. We may try to ignore the voice of conscience but it whispers to us that we have not done our best.

A Guilty Conscience Erodes Confidence

I have learned from experience that a guilty conscience hinders the flow of confidence. Confidence is faith in God and a belief that because He is helping you, you can succeed in whatever you need to do. However, if we feel guilty we will shrink back from God rather than boldly expecting Him to assist us. We will give up rather than face our challenges in life because we feel bad about ourselves.

A woman we will call Stephanie heard that a position was open in her company and she wanted to apply for it. She needed to make more money and liked the idea and the prestige of promotion. Stephanie asked her supervisor if she could interview for the new job and was told to be prepared the next day to do so. All that evening something was bothering Stephanie; she wasn't sure what it was but she had a vague fear that she would not get the job. When the time came the next day for the interview, she wasn't even sure she should apply. Her confidence disappeared and she wasn't looking forward to answering her supervisor's questions. During the interview, it was obvious that she wasn't sure of herself. When asked if she believed she could do the job, she replied, "I hope so." The minute her supervisor realized that Stephanie lacked confidence, she lost confidence in her also and quickly ended the interview. Stephanie later received a notice in her mailbox at work that someone else had filled the position.

Stephanie began praying about what had happened to her confidence. Why did she suddenly seem so unsure of herself? After a time of soul searching and prayer she remembered some things that had taken place in the past few months at work. She was making personal unnecessary phone calls during working hours knowing it was against company policy. Her conscience bothered her when she did it, but she reasoned that the company did not pay her enough anyway and she deserved a few perks. She also took extra long lunch hours on days when her supervisor was out of the office. Once again her conscience bothered her but she excused her behavior to herself and went on. The Bible tells us that reasoning leads us into deception that is contrary to the truth. The truth was plain and simple. Stephanie's actions were wrong! No reasoning or excuses could change that. She was stealing from her company and even though she tried to ignore her conscience, deep down inside she felt guilty about her actions. Now she understood why she could not apply with confidence for the position she desired. She learned that confidence and condemnation don't work well together.

If you want to walk confidently with assurance and your head held high, then strive to keep your conscience clear of offense toward God and man.

Even quitting when you know you should keep going will bother your conscience. God did not give us His Holy Spirit so we could be in bondage to fear. He did not send the power of His Spirit into our lives so we could be weak-willed, wimpy or the type of person who gives up when the going gets tough. Remember: God did not give us a spirit of fear, but of power, love and a sound mind (2 Timothy 1:7, KJV).

Opposition Will Always Be There

In the beginning of my ministry, God gave me a dream. In the dream, I was driving down a highway and I noticed cars pulling off. Some were parking and others were turning around to go back where they came from. I assumed there must be trouble up ahead but could not see what it was. As I boldly continued to drive forward I saw a bridge with water from the river below starting to flow across it. I realized that the people in the cars were afraid they might get hurt or get somewhere and not be able to get back. My dream ended with me sitting in my car looking first at the water-covered bridge, back where I had been, and to the side of the road, trying to decide if I should park, retreat or keep moving forward. Then I woke up.

God used that dream to show me that there will always be opposition when pressing toward a goal. There will always be opportunity to park and go no farther or turn around and give up. It was up to me to decide each time if I would give up or go on. That dream has helped me many times to press on when difficulties came and I was tempted to quit. I have decided that even though I don't always do everything right, and I may not always get the result that I hope for, I will never quit! Determination will get you a lot farther than talent. So if you feel you lack in talent, take heart. All you need to win in life is more determination than anyone else you know.

Chapter Sixteen

BECOME A COURAGEOUS WOMAN

All of us, at one time or another, wish we had more courage. Think about the courage that Jochebed, the mother of Moses, showed. She defied Pharoah's order to kill all of the Hebrew boys and hid her son for three months before finally placing him in a basket, praying and trusting that God would provide. Her daughter, Miriam, exhibited great courage when she watched her little brother's makeshift boat float right to Pharoah's daughter. Instead of hiding, or running away, she approached the Princess with boldness and offered to get a Hebrew nurse (Moses' mother) to help care for the child.

Courage means to be brave, bold, and adventurous. It's a quality like that in Jochebed and Miriam's example that allows a person to encounter danger and difficulty with firmness and resolve.

We all need courage. Courage comes from God while fear is what Satan tries to give us. I was always afraid until I developed a strong relationship with God. I pretended that I wasn't afraid, but I was.

In the Bible we see the phrase "take courage." Courage is available, the same way fear is, but we can choose to reject fear and take courage.

I have told you these things, so that in Me you may have [perfect] peace and confidence. In the world you have tribulation and trials and distress and frustration; but be of good cheer [take courage; be confident, certain, undaunted]! For I have overcome the world. [I have deprived it of power to harm you and have conquered it for you.] (John 16:33)

If you skipped over the Scripture just now, go back and read it. Look at each word and meditate on it so that you get the full meaning of what Jesus is saying. He is telling us that during our lives we will have hard times, trials, and things that frustrate us, but we don't have to let worry or depression be part of it because He has given us courage (if we will take it), confidence, and assurance. No matter what comes against us, if we have confidence that we can make it through, it won't bother us that much. It isn't really our problems that make us unhappy; it is how we respond to them.

When trials and tribulations come, Satan will offer fear but God offers faith, courage and confidence. Which one are you receiving? The answer to this question may reveal the root of many frustrations.

The book of Job says that what we fear comes upon us (Job 3:25). That is a sobering thought. Satan offers fear, and if we take it and meditate on it and talk about it long enough we give it creative power.

Also, notice what else Jesus said in the above passage from John 16:33: He says "be confident." Notice that He did not say, "feel confident." As I have said repeatedly in this book, we can choose to be confident, even if we don't feel confident at all. Start today choosing to be confident in every situation and you will begin driving fear back to Hades where it came from. When Satan tries to give you fear, give it back to him. You wouldn't drink poison if someone offered it to you, would you? Then stop taking fear and start choosing courage.

Discouragement

When I think of discouragement, I think of an oppressive spirit, one that extinguishes courage and deprives us of the confidence God wants us to have. Discouragement is certainly not from God, so it must be another one of the devil's offerings. God gives courage, the devil gives dis-courage. He may try to discourage us through repeated trials or aggravations. He tries to discourage us through people who tear us down instead of building us up. Negative people can discourage us.

Today I heard about a 42-year-old man with a family who went to the doctor with a backache and discovered he had cancer in several places in his body. His spirit remained "up" and he never lost courage until one doctor looked at him and said, "There is no hope." What a stupid thing to say. Now, I realize that legally a doctor has to tell a patient the true facts, but she could have said it in a way that wasn't quite so crude. Besides, there is always hope. There are no hopeless cases when a person has God on their side.

Don't spend time with people who tear you down and give you the worst case scenario about everything. It is much easier to stand in a chair and have someone pull you down then for you to pull that person up to stand with you. We must constantly be on our guard against discouragement.

Encouragement

The Duke of Wellington, the British military leader who defeated Napoleon at Waterloo, was not an easy man to serve under. He was brilliant, demanding, and not one to shower his subordinates with compliments. Yet even Wellington realized that his methods left something to be desired. In his old age a young lady asked him what, if anything, he would do differently if he had his life to live over again. Wellington thought for a moment, and then replied. "I'd give more praise," he said.[1]

> If a farmer plants tomato seeds, he will get a harvest of tomatoes. If we plant encouragement in the lives of other people, we will reap a harvest of encouragement in our own.

All of us need encouragement. It is a tool that increases our confidence and inspires us to act with courage, spirit or strength. That is what we need! We don't need anyone around to discourage us . . . instead we need "encouragers" in our life. The Bible instructs us to encourage and edify one another.

> *Therefore encourage [admonish, exhort] one another and edify [strengthen and build up] one another . . .* (I Thessalonians 5:11)

Because we all encounter difficulty while we are running our race and trying to reach our goals, we all need encouragement. The more we get, the easier it is to stay on track and avoid wasting days or weeks in depression and despair. One of the best ways I know to get something I want or need is to give some of it away. God's Word teaches us to sow and then we shall reap. If a farmer plants tomato seeds, he will get a harvest of tomatoes. If we plant encouragement in the lives of other people, we will reap a harvest of encouragement in our own.

What we make happen for someone else, God will make happen for us. Do you sometimes find yourself wishing you had more encouragement, maybe from your family, or your friends, or your boss? But how often do you encourage others? If you're not sure, then make an extra effort right away. You can be the channel that God uses to keep someone confidently pressing toward success rather than giving up. Did you know that the Holy Spirit is called The Encourager? The Greek word *parakletos* is translated as the word Holy Spirit and includes comfort, edification and encouragement as part of its definition. Through the Holy Spirit, Jesus sent us a Comforter, a Helper, a Strengthener, an Edifier, and an Encourager and He sent Him to be in close fellowship with us. He lives inside of those who are believers in Jesus Christ, and you cannot get much closer than that. Let God encourage you through His Spirit. He will never tell you that you're not going to make it. He will never tell you that your case is hopeless.

God corrects and chastises us when we need it, but He also encourages us along the way. This is how we should raise our children. As a matter of fact, Paul said in his letter to the Colossians that fathers were not to place undue and unnecessary chastisement on their children, lest it discourage them, make them feel inferior, frustrate them and break their spirits (Colossians 3:21). If God gives earthly fathers that instruction, then He certainly will be no different toward His children.

So please remember that when discouragement comes from any source, that it isn't God sending it your way! Immediately reject it and if you have no other source of encouragement, then do what David did. The Bible says that he encouraged himself in the Lord. When you feel yourself starting to lose courage, talk to yourself! Tell yourself that you have made it through difficulties in the past and you will make it again. Remind yourself of past victories. Make a list of your blessings and read them out loud anytime you feel yourself starting to sink emotionally.

One of the ways you can encourage yourself is to read stories of uncommon courage. When you see what others have done, it encourages you that you can do whatever you need to do.

Uncommon Courage

We are inspired by people with uncommon courage. They help bring the best out of us. When we hear the stories of others, it inspires and encourages us to do the same. Here is a collection of stories we can gain insight from. I hope they minister to you as much as they ministered to me.

They All Voted to Die

In the days of war a Japanese policeman who had absolute power said that within three days everyone in a certain For-mosan mountain village were required to come to the police station and swear against Christianity, or his hands and feet would be tied together, he would be weighed down with stones and thrown from the high bridge into the rushing river below.

The Christians met at midnight to decide what to do. Some said, "We'll have to give it up. We can't be Christians now. He will surely kill us."

Then a young boy stood up. "But don't you remember that Jesus said not to be afraid of those who can only kill the body, but to be afraid of those who kill body and soul? If he kills us, it will only be our bodies. Our souls will go to be with Jesus." They all said, "That is true." When the vote was taken, every hand was raised—all voted to die. The next day the policeman laughed cruelly, and said, "Tomorrow you die."

Now the policeman liked to fish, and waded out into the river. A rock or tree in the current struck his leg and broke it. While the mountain people were praying, a messenger rushed in, and said, "The man who was to kill you tomorrow has been drowned in the river."[2]

Was it a coincidence? I don't think so. When the village people chose boldness over fear, their faith in God opened a door for His deliverance. It is just like God to drown the enemy in the same river he planned to drown them in. Satan's plans backfire on him when we keep moving in faith and confidence.

Facing Down a Threat

A colonel of the Seventh Rhode Island Regiment, in the War Be-
tween the States, had become very unpopular with his men.
The report reached him that in the next engagement his own
regiment would look for opportunities to shoot him. When he
heard that, he gave orders for the men to march out for the
cleaning of their muskets; and taking position on top of a bank
of clay and facing the regiment, he gave the order "Ready!
Aim! Fire!" Any man could have killed him without the slight-
est risk of discovery; but every soldier admired his superb
courage, and whoever was disposed to kill him refrained.[3]

This colonel could have lived in tormenting fear that at any
time one of his men might shoot him. Instead, he chose to confront the threat head on and once again we see that courage wins.

We should not be afraid of threats. Satan likes to intimidate
people by threatening them with thoughts of bad things to come.
If we face threats boldly, quite often the enemy backs down. Bul-
lies can only bully those who won't confront them. No matter
what threatens us it can never separate us from the love of God.

If there's anything that sticks
with you after you put this
book down, please remember
this: Don't live in fear of what
may happen. Maybe you have
heard of a threat of a layoff at

> A great woman doesn't allow fear to
> be her master. She courageously
> looks it in the face and faces it down
> with God by her side.

work, or a stock market decline, or you may have gotten a bad report from the doctor. All these things can be subject to change.
Without a moment's notice God can change anything in our circumstances! Remain hopeful and don't let fear rule. Confront fear
and you will find it isn't as powerful as you thought it was. Remember, courage is not the absence of fear, but action in the presence
of it. There is no such thing as courage where fear is not present. A

great woman doesn't allow fear to be her master. She courageously looks it in the face and stares it down with God by her side.

Courage Despite Adversity

Paul Partridge lives in suburban Chicago. In a land mine in Vietnam in 1966, he lost both legs. He lived across the street from a woman who screamed one day at the top of her voice: "My baby! My baby!" Sensing there was something seriously wrong, this veteran and his wife left their house—he in his wheelchair, his wife running. After sixty bumpy yards, the wheelchair stopped. He dragged himself out of that wheelchair . . . and pulled himself sixty feet up steps to the deck around the swimming pool. There was a little girl. Her mother had pulled her from the pool where she had found her apparently dead . . . her little heart stopped. Partridge gave the child CPR and talked to her. "Little girl, you're going to live. You're going to make it. I know you're going to make it." Suddenly the child started breathing, and he screamed for medics to be called.[4]

That's the nobility the Lord has planted in this dust we call flesh. That's why He made us just a little lower than the angels, with the potential to risk our lives for other people—as this hero did for his country, and who with great anguish and agony dragged himself sixty feet up steps to save that little girl.

Partridge could have made a different choice when the woman screamed for help. He could have simply said, "I am a cripple, I can't do anything to help her." And had he said that, no one would think any less of him. In fact, most would agree with him. But he did the opposite because he is a man of uncommon courage. He inspires the rest of us to face our challenges without complaining and be less concerned about ourselves and more concerned about others.

Here is another similar story:

One summer morning, as Ray Blankenship prepared his break-fast, he gazed out the window and saw a small girl being swept along in the rain-flooded drainage ditch beside his Andover, Ohio, home. Blankenship knew that farther downstream, the ditch disappeared with a roar underneath a road and then emptied into the main culvert. Ray dashed out the door and raced along the ditch, trying to get ahead of the foundering child. Then he hurled himself into the deep, churning water. Blankenship surfaced and was able to grab the child's arm. They tumbled end over end. Within three feet of the yawning culvert, Ray's free hand felt something—possibly a rock—protruding from one bank. He clung desperately, but the tremendous force of the water tried to tear him and the child away. "If I can just hang on until help comes," he thought. He did better than that. By the time the fire-department rescuers arrived, Blankenship had pulled the girl to safety. Both were treated for shock. On April 12, 1989, Ray Blankenship was awarded the Coast Guard's Silver Lifesaving Medal. The award is fitting, for this selfless person was at even greater risk to himself than most people knew. Ray Blankenship can't swim.[5]

If we were not so busy trying to avoid personal pain, fear could not dominate our lives. Perhaps we should once and for all put ourselves in God's capable hands, telling Him that what happens to us is His concern, not ours. Our joy increases as we help other people, but we won't reach out to others very much if we are fearful of what will happen to us.

Caring for Others

Barbara Makuch paid dearly for her willingness to aid Jews in Nazi-occupied Poland. She helped two Jewish people find pro-tection in the boy's boarding school where she was a teacher.

One was a young Jewish boy who successfully passed himself off as a Christian Polish student. The second was a woman doctor who became the school cook. Although they lived on minimal means in a tiny apartment, Barbara and her mother accepted responsibility for a seven-year-old Jewish girl, left with them by the girl's desperate mother. Fearing detection in such a small community, Barbara took the girl on a dangerous journey to Lvov where she placed her in the safe shelter of a convent school.

In Lvov, Barbara joined her sister Halina in her work for the underground organization, Zegota, set up to aid Polish Jews in hiding. On a Zegota courier mission Barbara was caught and subsequently imprisoned, first in a notorious jail, later at the Ravensbruck concentration camp in Germany. During her years in prison and camp, Barbara faced the harshest test of courage and endurance. Remarkably, she not only survived but even managed to help save the lives of fellow inmates.[6]

Just think of it. Barbara could have feared for own safety and done nothing. I am sure that millions did just that. But, she was a woman with uncommon courage. She risked her own life for other people and the result was that many lives were spared.

My Life Is a Prayer

Mary Khoury was seventeen years old when she and her family were forced to their knees in front of their home in Damour, Lebanon during the Lebanese Civil War (1975–1992).

The leader of the Muslim fanatics who raided their village waved his pistol carelessly before their faces. His hatred for Christians burned in his eyes. "If you do not become a Muslim," he threatened, "you will be shot."

Mary knew Jesus was given a similar choice. "Give up your plan to save sinners, or You will be crucified." He chose the cross.

Mary's choice was similar. "I was baptized as a Christian, and His word came to me: 'Don't deny your faith.' I will obey Him. Go ahead and shoot." The sound of a gun from behind her echoed in the valley and Mary's body fell limply to the ground.

Two days later, the Red Cross came into her village. Of all her family, Mary was the only one still alive. But the bullet cut her spinal cord, leaving both her arms paralyzed. They were stretched out from her body and bent at the elbows, reminiscent of Jesus at His Crucifixion. She could do nothing with them.

"Everyone has a vocation," she said. "I can never marry or do any physical work. So I will offer my life for Muslims, like the one who cut my father's throat, cursed my mother and stabbed her, and then tried to kill me. My life will be a prayer for them."[7]

It takes uncommon courage to be willing to die for what you believe in, but it also takes uncommon courage to be willing to forgive and pray for your persecutors. In our world today multitudes are offended, angry, bitter and resentful. If more people had the courage to forgive it would make our world a better place.

Taking a Stand

He came walking up the aisle on little fat, brown legs, with serious determination in his eyes. I stopped speaking and the congregation was quiet as death. "You asked me what I would have done if I had been in the crowd when Jesus fell under the weight of His cross." He looked earnestly up at me. "Please, sir, I would have helped carry it." He was a Mexican lad eight years of age. His father was a miner and his mother was an outcast from decent society. I had been preaching on Simon of Cyrene; and when I asked the audience to determine in their own hearts their reaction to that scene, little Pedro moved toward me.

I lifted my arm and cried: "Yes, and if you had helped Him to carry His cross, the cruel Roman soldiers would have beaten down across your back with their whips until the blood ran down to your heels!" He never flinched. Meeting my look with one of cool courage, he gritted through clenched teeth: "I don't care. I would have helped Him carry it just the same."

Two weeks later, at the close of the service in the same building, I stood at the door, greeting people as they left. When Pedro came by, I patted him affectionately on the back. He shrank from me with a little cry. "Don't do that, my back is sore." I stood in astonishment. I had barely touched his shoulders. I took him into the cloak room and removed his shirt from his body. Crisscrossed from his neck to his waist were ugly, bloody welts. "Who did that?" I cried in anger. "Mother did it. She whipped me because I came to church."[8]

In our world today most people compromise rather than take a stand for what is right. Jesus said we would be persecuted for righteousness sake and most people are not up for that. Jesus also promised a reward; however, the majority of people want reward without commitment. If we do what God has asked us to do, we will get what He promised us we could have. Salvation is free and its only condition is, "believe," but the benefits of being a Christian do come with conditions. God simply said, "If you will, I will." Most Christians live far below their God-ordained destiny and privileges simply because they compromise rather than taking a stand.

Little Pedro felt it was right for him to go to church and he was willing to suffer in order to do the right thing. Very few adults would do what he did. This little boy was an up-and-coming world changer. People with uncommon courage change the world around them. They don't conform to the world; they change it and make it a better place to live.

Do you find yourself complaining about conditions in the world today? Ask yourself: "What am I doing to change it?" If your answer is nothing, then stop complaining and get to work! Take a stand. If you are the only one you know who is willing to do what is right, then you be the one who will make a difference. Yes, it may be a lonely walk, there may be persecution along the way, but the rewards are worth it. You will have the satisfaction of knowing that you lived your life fully and completely and refused to let fear be your master.

> If you are the only one you know who is willing to do what is right, then you be the one who will make a difference.

Do All That You Can Do

Some individuals pass quietly and fearfully through life and never do anything to make the world a better place. They are so concerned with self-preservation that they never reach out to the millions of souls around them who are crying out for help. Just think about it . . . The woman at work whose fourteen-year-old son is killed in a drive-by shooting. The man whose wife leaves him for another man. The neighbor who just found out she has terminal cancer. Then there is the family you heard about at church who is in danger of losing their home because the husband lost his job and hasn't been able to find one for five months. The bank is ready to foreclose on their loan and they really have no where else to go. They are desperate and don't know what to do. Everyone tells them that God will provide, but no one is doing anything.

We must realize that God works through people. We are His hands, feet, arms, mouth, eyes and ears. God does miracles, but He does them through people with uncommon courage. Those who forget about themselves long enough will notice that God has placed someone in their path that is hurting and needy. We pray for God to use us and when He tries we are often too busy to be bothered.

When God created Adam and Eve, He blessed them, told them to be fruitful and multiply and use all the vast resources of the earth that He gave them in the service of God and man. Are you being fruitful? Is your life causing increase? When you get involved with people and things, do they increase and multiply? Some people only take in life, and they never add anything. I refuse to be that kind of person. I want to make people's lives better. I want to put smiles on faces. Are you using the resources you have in the service of God and man? We must all make sure that we are not like the rich man in the Bible who had so much that all of his barns were full with no room for more. Instead of giving any of it away, he decided that he would tear down the barns he had and just build bigger ones and collect more stuff for himself. I think he was the dumbest man in the Bible.

He could have decided that he would use what he had to bless others, but he must have been a fearful, selfish man, who only had room in his life for himself (Luke 12:16–20). God called the man a fool, and said, "This very night they (the messengers of God) will demand your soul of you; and all the things that you have prepared, whose will they be?" The man was going to die that night and all he would leave behind was "stuff." He had an opportunity to make the world a better place. He could have added to many lives and put smiles on thousands of faces. Instead, he fearfully and selfishly only cared about himself.

Be courageous. Forget about yourself and start doing all you can to help others. Get a new goal. . . . "Put smiles on faces." Encourage, edify, lift up, comfort, help, give hope, relieve pain, and lift burdens.

Jesus said if we want to be His disciples we will forget about ourselves, lose sight of ourselves and all of our own interests (Mark 8:34). The minute we hear that, fear strikes our hearts and we hear loudly in our heads, "what about me?" If I forget myself, who is going to take care of me? My beloved, do not be afraid, God Himself will take care of you. Everything you do for other people will come back to you many times over, with joy. If you are willing to give yourself away, you will have a much better life than you ever would have had trying to keep yourself.

Women are sensitive to the needs of others. They are discerning, they notice things. I believe God gives you and I an ability to be touched by the infirmities of others for the express purpose of helping. Women are experts in bringing comfort. Courageous women are givers. Don't just selfishly and fearfully pass through this life, but do everything you can, every way you can, for everyone that you can, as often as you can. If that is your goal, you will be one of those rare individuals who actually make the world a better place and put a smile on every face.

Chapter Seventeen

YOU GO GIRL!

I have shared a lot of what I know about how you can become a confident woman, and now I believe you are going to act on this information and begin living boldly and fearlessly. It doesn't matter how you lived before now, this is a new beginning. Every day God's mercy is new and it is available for all of us today. Don't look back, look forward!

Be decisive, follow your heart and don't be overly concerned about what other people think of you and your decisions. Most of them are not thinking about you as much as you might imagine that they are anyway.

Don't live constantly comparing yourself with others; be your unique self. (See Corinthians 10:12.) Celebrate who God has made you to be. There is only one who has the unique traits and skills that make up who you are. Enjoy the fact that God knew what He was doing and rely on the thought that surely God said the same thing about you as He did when He called the world into creation. "And it was good."

Confident Talk and a Confident Walk

So many times our outward appearance shows the way we're feeling inside. But it can also work the other way! When we look confident on the outside, we can feel more confident on the inside. When you walk, stand upright. Don't slump your shoulders and hang your head down. You are full of the life of God so act like it!

Live with passion, zeal and enthusiasm. Don't just try to "make it" through the day. Celebrate the day. Say, "This is the day the Lord has made, I will rejoice and be glad in it." (Psalm 118:24). Don't dread the day, attack the day. Know what you want to accomplish today and go for it.

Smile

It's a fact that's often stated, but it's worth mentioning here. It only takes seventeen muscles to smile, but forty-three to frown. In other words, you work a whole lot harder looking sour than looking happy! So make it a point to smile more. Smile a lot. The more you smile the better you will feel. Your smile not only makes you appear and feel more confident, it gives others confidence. They feel approved of and accepted when we smile at them. We actually say more with our body language than we do with words. I can often tell if a person is confident just by the way they carry themselves and by the look on their face. Some people always look unsure and even frightened, while others appear confident and at ease.

You may think that you cannot do anything about the way you look, but you can. I started out as a person who rarely smiled. I was abused and had a lot of disappointment in my life so I had a perpetual solemn look. I was actually secretly waiting for the next disaster to take place in my life. I had lost hope, I had a negative attitude, I was fearful and it showed on my face and in the way I carried myself. I started making changes by just smiling. Now I smile a lot.

Did you know that a smile is a wonderful weapon? It's so powerful you can break ice with it! If a person is cold toward you, just start smiling and see them warm up. If you wear a smile you will have friends, if you wear a frown all you will have is wrinkles. Smiles are a language that even babies understand. Smiles are multi-lingual; they are understood in every language. I heard some-one once say, "you are not fully dressed until you put on your smile."

Smiling actually makes you feel better and lifted up. Studies show that when you smile, your heart rate can actually lower and your breathing slows down, particularly if you're feeling stressed. When you get out of bed, even if you don't feel like smiling, force yourself to smile anyway and you will have a happier day. A smile of encouragement at the right moment may be the turning point for a troubled life. A smile costs nothing, but gives much. If you are not smiling, you are like a millionaire who has money in the bank, but no checks.

Most women are concerned about their looks and a smile is an inexpensive way to improve your looks instantly. Ziggy said, "a smile is a facelift that is in everyone's price range."

When you were born you were crying and everyone around you was smiling; live your life in such a way that when you die you will be smiling and everyone else will be crying.

You may be familiar with Joel Osteen, a pastor from Houston, Texas. Joel has become very popular in a short period of time. He not only pastors the largest church in the United States but he is also on television in many parts of the world. Joel is known as "the smiling preacher." He literally smiles all the time. I have eaten with him several times and I am still trying to figure out how he can eat and smile at the same time, but he does it. He is a great pastor and teacher of God's word, but I believe one of the main things that helps his popularity is his smile. People want to feel better and anytime we smile at them it helps them do that. A smile reassures people and puts them at ease.

Confident Talk

According to the Bible, the power of life and death is in the tongue and we often have to eat our words.

Death and life are in the power of the tongue, and they who in-dulge in it shall eat the fruit of it [for death or life].
(Proverbs 18:21)

I wonder how many times in our lives we say, "I'm afraid . . ." "I'm afraid I'll get that flu that is going around." "I'm afraid my kids will get in trouble." "I'm afraid it's going to snow, and I'm afraid to drive in it, if it does." "With the way prices are going up, I'm afraid I won't have enough money." "I'm afraid if I don't go to that party, people will think badly of me." "I'm afraid we won't get a good seat at the theater." "I'm afraid someone will break into my house while I'm out of town." If we heard a recording of every time in our life we have said, "I'm afraid," we would probably be amazed that our lives are going as well as they are.

If we really understood the power in words, I think we would change the way we talk. Our talk should be confident and bold, not fearful. Fearful talk not only affects us in an adverse way, but it affects those around us.

I want to make a bold statement right now. If you will just change the way you talk, you will immediately begin to feel stronger, bolder, courageous and less afraid. James said the tongue is like a wild beast and cannot be tamed by anyone (James 3:2–10). We certainly need God's help for this one! We are so accustomed to saying things without paying any attention at all to what we are saying, that we will need God's help just to recognize fearful, silly, foolish and sinful talk.

Even after we recognize the error of our ways we still need to form new habits. Making and breaking habits take time so don't get discouraged with yourself if you don't have immediate victory in this area. Keep at it and little by little you will develop the habit of saying things that add to your life, not take away from it.

Speak Life to Yourself

I am a great fan of speaking God's Word out loud. I even wrote a book on this subject called *The Secret Power of Speaking God's Word*. In the book I list Scriptures in categories, and present them as first-person confessions that make it easier for people to begin doing it.

Don't talk about yourself according to the way you feel or look. Speak God's Word over your life. Don't say about yourself what others say unless what they say is worth repeating. Perhaps your parents spoke to you in a way that caused you to lack confidence. They may not have known any better, but the good news is, you don't have to be affected by their words for the rest of your life. You can change your image of yourself beginning right now!

Don't say things like: "I just don't have any confidence," or, "I'll never overcome my fears." Say what you want, not what you have. Anything God says you can have, you can have. But you will need to get into agreement with Him. David said, "My confidence is in the Lord," and you can say the same thing. Paul said, "We can do all things through Christ who strengthens us." So you can say, "I can do whatever God tells me to do in life because Christ will give me strength." God says in His Word that He did not give us a spirit of fear, so we can say, "I will not fear, God has not given me a spirit of fear." I'm sure you get the idea by now.

As you speak God's Word out loud you renew your own mind. Remember, Romans 12 teaches us that though God has a good plan for our lives, we must totally renew our minds and learn how to think right before we will see it come to pass.

What is in your heart comes out of your mouth (Matthew 12:34) and what you keep in your mouth affects your heart. It is a cycle. What comes first, is it thoughts or words? It really doesn't matter because they affect each other and both must be corrected in order for us to enjoy the life Jesus died to give us.

Stop saying, "I'm depressed, I'm discouraged, "I'm ready to give

up" or "nothing good ever happens to me." All talk of that
type is totally useless. They are
words that cannot add to your
life, but they can certainly prevent you from living.

If we really understood the power that is in words, I think we would change the way we talk.

If you have considered yourself to be a person with low self-
esteem, no confidence, cowardly, timid, shy and fearful, I believe
this is a turning point for you. However, you will have to be per-
sistent. It is not what we do right one or two times that makes a
difference in our life; it's what we do right consistently.

Confident Talk Rubs Off

When you speak confidently it rubs off on others around you.
They will be confident in you if you sound like you're confident in
yourself. Don't be arrogant, but do be confident.

There is a woman who works in my office and she is the type of
woman that just seems to be able to do anything you ask her to do.
I don't know if she is as confident as she sounds, but she puts me
at ease. Anytime we ask her to do something her immediate response is "no problem." She doesn't mean it in an arrogant way,
she is simply saying that she will get it done and we don't have to
be concerned about it any longer. Busy people like me need people
like that in their life.

I am convinced that even if she didn't know how to do something, she would find out. Or she would get someone else to do it
who did know how. Another thing she frequently says when asked
to do something is, "I'll take care of it," and, she always does.

I am not suggesting that people try to do things they are not
gifted for and just fake it. Obviously, we need to do what God enables us to do, but we need to do it confidently. I am confident that
I am a very good Bible teacher. If I wasn't, then I really should not

> We cannot ask fearfully and expect to receive. We must come to God's throne boldly.

be trying to teach. What is the point in doing something all of your life if you believe that you aren't any good at it?

You go girl—you start talking and walking with confidence! It is time for you to look up, not down. It is time for you to expect great things to happen in your life.

Have a Confident Expectation

We have no right to expect what we have not prayed for. The Bible says we have not because we fail to ask (James 4:2). So ask and keep on asking (Matthew 7:7).

How you ask is also important. The Bible says in James 5:16 that the fervent, effectual prayer of a righteous man makes tremendous power available. What kind of man? A righteous man! Not one who feels guilty, condemned, no good, and as if God is angry with him. Not one who is fearful, cowardly, timid, indecisive and double-minded.

Doesn't the Bible say that our righteousness is like filthy rags and that all have sinned and come short of the glory of God. Yes, it does say that. But it is not our own righteousness that we wear into the prayer closet, it is the righteousness of Jesus Christ. It is that which is given to every true believer in Him.

He took our sins to the cross with Him and gave us His righteousness (2 Corinthians 5:21). We can call ourselves righteous women because He gives us right standing with God through His blood sacrifice.

We cannot ask fearfully and expect to receive. We must come to God's throne boldly. Several Scriptures tell us to do exactly that.

Let us then fearlessly and confidently and boldly draw near to the throne of grace [the throne of God's unmerited favor to

us sinners], that we may receive mercy [for our failures] and
find grace to help in good time for every need [appropriate
help and well-times help, coming just when we need it].
(Hebrews 4:16)

We see from this Scripture the attitude we should come with. Fearless! Confident! Bold! We come in that way because we know with assurance that God is faithful, He is Good, and He wants to meet our needs.

We don't need to act as if God is a miser and that we must twist His arm and try to convince Him to help us. He is waiting to hear your cry!

Some people are unable to pray boldly because their consciences bother them. There are things they need to repent of and commitments they need to make to do things differently. If that is the case with you, then just do it. If something is wrong in your life, don't spend the rest of your days feeling bad about it . . . do something about it!

And, beloved, if our consciences [our hearts] do not accuse us
[if they do not make us feel guilty and condemn us], we have
confidence [complete assurance and boldness] before God.
(I John 3:21)

Ephesians 3:20 tells us that God is able to do exceedingly, abundantly, above and beyond all that we could ever dare to hope, ask or think. Are you daring in prayer? Are you expecting enough? The devil wants us to believe we must go to God with head hung low, telling Him how terrible we are. He wants us to believe that we dare not ask for too much, because after all, we don't deserve anything. Satan is afraid of bold, daring, confident, fearless and expectant prayer.

I love the Scripture I am about to quote so please take time to look it over carefully.

In Whom, because of our faith in Him, we dare to have the boldness [courage and confidence] of free access [an unreserved approach to God with freedom and without fear].
(Ephesians 3:12)

WOW! WOW! and, another WOW! We have free access. We can go before God anytime we want to. We don't need a special invitation. The throne room is always open, God is always home, He is never napping or on the phone. We can go boldly, expecting Him to meet our need and do it willingly and joyfully.

No doubt millions of people pray, but the question we want answered is, how do they pray? Do they pray expectantly, boldly, fearlessly, confidently, aggressively, or, ashamed, condemned, asking for barely enough to get by on, and seriously doubting if they will even get that?

You go girl! Start praying like you have never prayed before. Believe that God wants to meet your needs because He is good, not necessarily because you are good. None of us living in a fleshly body has a perfect record, we all make mistakes and yours probably are no worse than anyone else's. So, stop beating up on yourself and start expecting God to be God in your life.

BE confident even when you don't FEEL confident and watch God work!

It's a New Day

Many of the wrong attitudes toward women have either changed or they are in the process of being changed. We still have a way to go, but as the saying goes, "we've come a long way, baby!" As I said earlier, we appreciate the women who pioneered the women's rights movement. We are sorry for the women who lived in the past and did not know the freedom we enjoy today. We mourn the memory of the millions of women throughout history who were robbed of their God-given destinies. If for no other reason, we must press forward and be all we can be for them.

You go girl! It is a new day. There are no hindrances. The door is wide open for you to realize your dreams. Walk confidently into your future and never look back!

END NOTES

INTRODUCTION

1. Greenberg, Susan H. & Anna Kuchment "The Family Moon." *Newsweek*, Jan. 9, 2006, page 47.
2. *Parenting*, Feb. 2006, page 100.
3. *Parenting*, ibid, page 99.
4. *Newsweek*, ibid, page 98.
5. *Parenting*, ibid, page 98.
6. ibid, page 98.
7. ibid, page 30.
8. ibid, page 30.
9. ibid, page 29.
10. ibid, page 100.
11. *Parenting*, Feb. 2006, page 100.

CHAPTER 1. CONFIDENCE

1. *God's Little Devotional Book for the Workplace,* by Todd Hafer. Colorado Springs: Honor Books, 2001. Pages 310–311.
2. www.en.wikipedia.org/wiki/Golden_Gate_Bridge. last accessed 6/15/06
3. *Daily Grace for Teens,* by Richard Baxter, Brother Andrew, et. al, Colorado Springs: Honor Books, 2005.
4. Charles Swindoll, Kindred Spirit, Vol. 22, No. 3, Autumn, 1998, p. 3.
5. *God's Little Devotional Book for the Workplace*, by Todd Hafer. Colorado Springs: Honor Books, 2001. pp. 182–183.
6. "The Journal of John Wesley," *www.ccel.org/ccel/wesley/journal. toc.html.* Last accessed 6/16/06.

CHAPTER 2. SETTING THE RECORD STRAIGHT

1. Loren Cunningham, David Joel Hamilton, with Janice Rogers. *Why Not Women: A Fresh Look at Scripture on Women in Missions, Ministry and Leadership*. Seattle: YWAM Publishing, 2000. Pg. 17.
2. Cunningham, Hamilton, p.72.
3. Cunningham, Hamilton, p. 73
4. "Trafficking In Persons Report," The Office to Monitor and Combat Trafficking in Persons, U.S. Department of State, June 3, 2005. *http://www.state.gov/g/tip/rls/tiprpt/2005/46606.htm*. Last accessed 6/16/06.
5. ibid
6. "Female genital circumcision: medical and cultural considerations," Cindy M. Little. *Journal of Cultural Diversity*, Spring 2003.
7. "2004 National Crime Victimization Survey." The Rape, Abuse & Incest National Network (RAINN). *http://www.rainn.org/statistics/*. Last accessed 6/16/06.
8. "Criminal Victimization, 2003." Washington, DC: Bureau of Justice Statistics, U.S. Department of Justice. *www.ojp.usdoj.gov/bjs/abstract/cv03.htm. Last accessed 6/16/06.*
9. ibid
10. *In Her Own Right: The Life of Elizabeth Cady Stanton*, by Elisabeth Griffith. New York: Oxford University Press, 1984.
11. The U.S. Census Bureau reported in the 2005 Current Population Survey Annual Social and Economic Supplement that real median earnings of men age 15 and older who worked full-time, year-round declined 2.3 percent between 2003 and 2004, to $40,798. Women with similar work experience saw their earnings decline by 1.0 percent, to $31,223. Reflecting the larger fall in the earnings of men, the ratio of female-to-male earnings for full-time, year-round workers was 77 cents on the dollar, up from 76 cents in 2003.

CHAPTER 4. SEVEN SECRETS OF A CONFIDENT WOMAN

1. *www.sermonillustrations.com/a-z/f/faith.htm*. Last accessed 6/20/06.

CHAPTER 6. OVERCOMING SELF-DOUBT

1. *Reader's Digest,* Oct., 1991, p. 62.
2. Barbara L. Fredrickson, "The Value of Positive Emotions: The Emerging Science of Positive Psychology Is Coming to Understand Why It's Good to Feel Good." *American Scientist,* Vol. 91, July-August 2003. Article mentions a study that was performed that monitored the feelings and attitudes of a group of Catholic nuns back in the 1930s which discovered that "the nuns who expressed the most positive emotions lived up to 10 years longer than those who expressed the fewest."

CHAPTER 7. THE POWER OF PREPARATION

1. RWD, "Grass on Your Path," *Our Daily Bread,* November 18, 1996.
2. " 'Entitlement Generation' expects it all'," Patricia Breakey, The Daily Star, July 2, 2005. *www.thedailystar.com/news/stories/2005/07/02/gen1.html.* Last accessed 6/16/06

CHAPTER 8. WHEN THE WORLD SAYS NO

1. "No More Ms. Nice Guy! Confessions of a Recovering People Pleaser." Nancy Kennedy. *Today's Christian Woman,* November/December 2002, Vol. 24, No. 6, Page 70.
2. "A Quick Biography of Benjamin Franklin," *www.ushistory.org/franklin/info/index.htm.* Last accessed 6/16/06
3. "Alexander Graham Bell-Biography," *http://inventors.about.com/library/inventors/bltelephone2.htm.* Last accessed 6/16/06.
4. "Semmelweiss, Ignaz Philipp," *http://www.answers.com/topic/ignaz-semmelweis.* Last accessed 6/16/06.
5. "Margaret Knight—Queen of Paper Bags," by Mary Bellis, *http://inventors.about.com/library/inventors/blknight.htm.* Last accessed 6/16/06.
6. "Female Inventors: Hedy Lamarr." *http://www.inventions.org/culture/female/lamarr.html.* Last accessed 6/16/06.
7. "Getting What You Deserve," by Steve Goodier. *http://www.inspirationalstories.com.* Last accessed 6/16/06.

CHAPTER 9. ARE WOMEN REALLY THE WEAKER SEX?

1. "U.S. Census Bureau Report." *www.census.gov*. Last accessed 6/16/06.
2. *A Box of Delights*, compiled by J. John and Mark Stibbe, Canada: Monarch Books, 2002, pg. 121.
3. *Bartlett's Familiar Quotations*, eds. John Bartlett and Justine Kaplan. Boston: Little, Brown and Company, 1996 pgs. 144–145.
4. ibid, p. 654.
5. *100 Women Who Shaped History*. Gail Meyer Rolks, San Francisco: Bluewood Books, 1994.
6. *World Book Encyclopedia* Chicago: Chicago World Book, Inc. 1996, p. 275.
7. *www.brainyquotes.com/quotesauthors/m/margaret_thatcher.html*. Last accessed 6/19/06.
8. *100 Women Who Shaped History*. Gail Meyer Rolks, San Francisco: Bluewood Books, 1994.
9. *International Dictionary of Women's Biography*. The Continuum Publishing Co., 1982.
10. Stowe, Harriet Beecher, Uncle Tom's Cabin, (New York: Signet Classic 1966) pgs. v-vi, 20–21
11. *www.webster.edu/~woolflm/dorotheadix.html*. Last accessed 6/19/06.
12. *World Book Encyclopedia*. Chicago: World Book, Inc. 1996. pp. 171–172.
13. "Yes, Women Are Different from Men," by Jane Everhart. *International Journal of Humanities and Peace*, Vol. 16, 2000. p. 96.
14. *Love and Respect*. Dr. Emerson Eggerichs, Nashville: Integrity Publishers, 2004, pg. 30.
15. *For Women Only* by Shaunti Feldhahn, Sisters: Multnomah Publishers, Inc. 2004. pg. 25.
16. Sparks, quoted in *Homemade*, Dec. 1984. Accessed at: *www.bible.org/illus.asp?topic_id=1695*. 6/19/06.

CHAPTER 10. STEPS TO INDEPENDENCE

1. Scarf, Maggie. *Unfinished Business: Pressure Points in the Lives of Women*. New York: Doubleday, 1980.
2. Barbara Hatcher, *Vital Speeches*, March 1, 1987. Accessed at: *http://www.sermonillustrations.com/a-z/s/speech.htm*. 6/20/06.

3. "Engaging Your Employees." James K. Clifton, SHRM Online. *www.shrm.org/foundation/engaging.asp*. Last accessed 6/19/06.
4. "How a Country Music Superstar Found Her Real Self," by Carol Crenshaw, December 1, 2005. *www.wynonna.com*. Last accessed 6/19/06.

CHAPTER 11. THE ANATOMY OF FEAR

1. "The Numbers Count: Mental Disorders in America," National Institute of Mental Health. *http://www.nimh.nih.gov*. Last accessed 6/19/06.
2. *Confidence Booster Workout* by Martin Perry. Berkeley, CA: Thunder Bay Press, 2004.
3. "Runaway bride's pastor to publish book on 'foolish decisions.'" Greg Bluestein. *The Macon Telegraph*, Jan. 6, 2006. *http://www. macon.com*. Last accessed 6/20/06.
4. *Our Daily Bread*, April 6, 1995. Accessed at: *http://www.iclnet. org/pub/resources/text/Our.Daily.Bread/db950406.txt*. 6/20/06.
5. *Caring Enough to Confront* by David Augsburger, Ventura, CA: Regal, 1980.
6. Story from Dr. Jeff Ginn who serves as pastor of the Mount Pleasant Baptist Church, Colonial Heights, Va.
7. *www.cybernation.com/quotationcenter*. Last accessed 6/19/06.

CHAPTER 12. FEAR HAS RELATIVES

1. "Teenage girls suffer in silence. They really are worried sick." The Observer. June 28, 1998. Accessed at: *http://www.childrens-express.org/dynamic/public/d299901.htm*. 6/19/06.
2. *Preacher's Commentar #26: Luke* by Bruce Larson, Nashville: Nelson Reference and E-publications, 2003. p. 43
3. *www.cyberntion.org/quotationcenter*. Last accessed 6/19/06.
4. *Hell's Best Kept Secret*, by Ray Comfort, New Kensington: Whitaker House, 1989. pp. 160–161.
5. Adapted from *The Great Stories CD*, John Ortberg, South Barrington, Il.

CHAPTER 13. THE RELATIONSHIP BETWEEN STRESS AND FEAR

1. *Surviving Information Overload* by Kevin A. Miller, Grand Rapids, MI: Zondervan, 2004. pg. 27.
2. "The Life of Henry Ford." *http://www.hfmgv.org/exhibits/hf/default.asp.* Last accessed 6/19/06.
3. "People & Discoveries: Jonas Salk 1914–1995," *http://www.pbs. org/wgbh/aso/databank/entries/bmsalk.html.* Last accessed 6/19/06.
4. *Bits & Pieces*, April 29, 1993. p. 3
5. Howard Hendricks, in *The Monday Morning Mission.* Accessed at: *www.sermonillustrations.com/a-z/c/change.htm.* 6/19/06.

CHAPTER 14. CHOSSING BOLDNESS

1. *Victory in the Valleys of Life* by Charles Allen, Old Tappan: Revell, 1981.

CHAPTER 15.WINNERS NEVER QUIT

1. *www.cybernation.com/quotationcenter.* Last accessed 6/19/06.

CHAPTER 16. BECOME A COURAGEOUS WOMAN

1. *Bits & Pieces*, March 31, 1994, p.24. Accessed at: *www.bible.org/ illus.asp.* 6/19/06.
2. "Courage: They All Voted to Die," in *Child Evangelism.* Accessed at: *www.elbourne.org/sermons/index.mv?illustration+3928.* 6/19/06.
3. "Courage: Facing Down a Threat" by McCartney. Accessed at: *www.elbourne.org/sermons/index.mv?illustration+3925.* 6/19/06.
4. "Courage." Accessed at: *www.elbourne.org/sermons/index.mv?illus- tration+1285.* 6/19/06.
5. Paul Harvey, Los Angeles Times Syndicate. Accessed at: *www.ser- monillustrations.com/a-z/c/courage.htm.* 6/19/06.
6. "To Save a Life: Stories of the Holocaust Rescue," Story synopsis, The Barbara Makuch Story. Accessed at: *www.humboldt.edu/~res- cuers/book/synopses.html.* 6/19/06.

7. *In the Face of Surrender: Over 200 Challenging and Inspiring Stories of Overcomers* by Richard Wurmbrand, New Brunswick, NJ: Bridge-Logos Publishers, 1998. pp. 219–220.
8. Told by Harold Dye, in *The Teacher*. Accessed at: *http://elbourne.org/sermons/index.mv?illustration+3930.* 6/20/06.

JOYCE MEYER is one of the world's leading practical Bible teachers. A #1 *New York Times* bestselling author, she has written more than eighty inspirational books, including *100 Ways to Simplify Your Life, Never Give Up!*, the entire Battlefield of the Mind family of books, and two novels, *The Penny* and *Any Minute*, as well as many others. She has also released thousands of audio teachings, as well as a complete video library. Joyce's *Enjoying Everyday Life*® radio and television programs are broadcast around the world, and she travels extensively conducting conferences. Joyce and her husband, Dave, are the parents of four grown children and make their home in St. Louis, Missouri.

JOYCE MEYER MINISTRIES
U.S. & FOREIGN OFFICE ADDRESSES

Joyce Meyer Ministries
P.O. Box 655
Fenton, MO 63026
USA
(636) 349-0303
www.joycemeyer.org

Joyce Meyer Ministries—Canada
P.O. Box 7700
Vancouver, BC V6B 4E2
Canada
(800) 868-1002

Joyce Meyer Ministries—Australia
Locked Bag 77
Mansfield Delivery Centre
Queensland 4122
Australia
(07) 3349 1200

Joyce Meyer Ministries—England
P.O. Box 1549
Windsor SL4 1GT
United Kingdom
01753 831102

Joyce Meyer Ministries—South Africa
P.O. Box 5
Cape Town 8000
South Africa
(27) 21-701-1056

The Secrets of Spiritual Power

The Battle Belongs to the Lord

The Secrets to Exceptional Living

Eight Ways to Keep the Devil Under Your Feet

Teenagers Are People Too!

Filled with the Spirit

Celebration of Simplicity

The Joy of Believing Prayer

Never Lose Heart

Being the Person God Made You to Be

A Leader in the Making

"Good Morning, This Is God!" (gift book)

Jesus—Name Above All Names

Making Marriage Work
(Previously published as *Help Me—I'm Married!*)

Reduce Me to Love

Be Healed in Jesus' Name

How to Succeed at Being Yourself

Weary Warriors, Fainting Saints

Be Anxious for Nothing*

Straight Talk Omnibus

Don't Dread

Managing Your Emotions

Healing the Brokenhearted

Me and My Big Mouth!*

Prepare to Prosper

Do It Afraid!

Expect a Move of God in Your Life . . . Suddenly!

*Enjoying Where You Are on the
Way to Where You Are Going*

A New Way of Living

When, God, When?

Why, God, Why?

The Word, the Name, the Blood

Tell Them I Love Them

Peace

*If Not for the Grace of God**

JOYCE MEYER SPANISH TITLES

*Las Siete Cosas Que Te Roban el Gozo
(Seven Things That Steal Your Joy)
Empezando Tu Dia Bien (Starting Your Day Right)*

* Study Guide available for this title.

BOOKS BY DAVE MEYER

Life Lines